Oriental Architecture/2

Mario Bussagli

Oriental Architecture/2

China, Korea, Japan

Translated by John Shepley

Contributions by
Paola Mortari Vergara,
Chiara Silvi Antonini,
Adolfo Tamburello

Electa/*Rizzoli*
NEW YORK

Photographs: Federico Borromeo
Drawings: Studio Enzo di Grazia
Layout: Arturo Anzani

Library of Congress Cataloging in Publication Data

Bussagli, Mario.
    Oriental architecture.

    (History of world architecture)
    Translation of: Architettura orientale.
    Bibliography: p.
    Includes index.
    Contents: 1. India, Indonesia, Indochina —
2. China, Korea, Japan.
    1. Architecture, Oriental. I. Title. II. Series:
History of world architecture (Electa/Rizzoli)
NA1460.B8713   1989   722   88-43458
ISBN 0-8478-1056-9 (v. 1) (pbk.)
ISBN 0-8478-1055-0 (v. 2) (pbk.)

This volume is the redesigned paperback
of the original Italian edition published in 1973
by Electa, S.p.a., Milan,
and the English edition published
by Harry N. Abrams, Inc., New York

Printed in Italy

TABLE OF CONTENTS

Introduction

We wish to point out, first of all, that our title, "Himalayan Region," does not correspond in any way to the present political situation of the region we are about to consider. It has instead been chosen for geographical and historical reasons. Kashmir, Nepal, and Tibet occupy within the Himalayan chain a position that has endowed them with common characteristics, and they have shared for more or less brief periods similar vicissitudes. We must take into account also that from the religious and artistic standpoint these three countries—at least upon their emergence on the plane of civilization as we know it—found a common matrix in historical India.

Obviously, the Indian influence did not prevent the Himalayan world from developing independently the plastic and figurative arts, but constitutes instead the model to which we will have to refer often if we are to understand the historical and artistic events of Kashmir, Nepal, and Tibet. In the architectural sphere, this phenomenon is particularly evident in such religious monuments as the stupa, monastery, and Hindu temple. Since these structures were intended to discharge a given function—precisely that of the cult—a display of determined elements of construction is inevitable. We will thus have similar structures in a world where, unlike the West, the symbolic value is much more important than the aesthetic one. Of course artistic sensibility and religious symbolism change from region to region due to different influences and varying geographical and historical conditions; there exists also a local substratum that does not always spontaneously allow a transition to the claims and conditioning effects of new cultures. We cannot, therefore, expect these similar structures to be identical.

On the other hand, the panorama of so-called lay or civil architecture is more varied, even though it too—and perhaps to the same degree—is governed by elements extrinsic to pure aesthetic value and is subject to laws that keep it closely tied to political, economic, and/or military factors.

In this chapter, which is proposed essentially as a history of monuments in the Himalayan region, we will therefore follow the two strands representing religious and civil constructions—given the limits (unfortunately still fairly narrow even today) set by present-day archaeological research and scientific studies.

Kashmir

The name Kashmir (*Kasmira* in Sanskrit) indicates the region comprising the valley of the Jhelum River and its tributaries, as well as the inner slopes of the mountain chains that determine its boundaries. The geographical position of Kashmir, a pleasant and fertile valley completely surrounded by mountains, helped in the past to protect it from all-too-frequent aggression, and at the same time to isolate it partially from the outside world. Its fortunate physical situation had considerable importance in the course of the historical vicissitudes through which the country passed. Insofar as architecture is concerned, it contributed to no small degree to the creation

3. Vantipur, temple of Avantisvami: a) plan; b) plan and elevation of the peristyle (Enciclopedia Universale dell'Arte).

4. Vantipur, temple of Avantisvara.

5. Vantipur, temple of Avantisvara, detail.

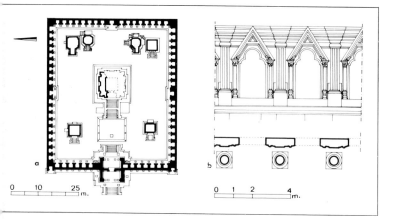

creature and eventually they succeeded. When they drained the lake that had been his home, they brought to light the verdant valley that we know today as Kashmir.

The chronicler Kalhana, in compiling the *Rajatarangini* (the dynastic chronicle of Kashmir), places a series of fifty-two kings, who must also be considered of legendary origin, at the beginning of Kashmir's history. Historical outlines begin to emerge more precisely with the appearance of a ruler by the name of Gonandiya III. The Gonandiya dynasty was destined to survive until the later advent of the Karkota dynasty; its duration is not specified by Kalhana and cannot be deduced from other sources. It appears, however, that Kashmir was part of the Maurya Empire during the reign of the great Asoka, and of the Kushan Empire; Kanishka, the most famous Kushan ruler, is reported to have sponsored in Kashmir the second great Buddhist council recorded in the sacred texts. Unfortunately, it would later fall into the hands of the Hephthalites, the people Buddhist sources blame for huge massacres and destruction in the whole northwest territory of India, which suffered harsh domination under these so-called White Huns.

Finally, in A.D. 622, Durlabhavardhana founded the Karkota dynasty, whose most illustrious representative was to be Lalitaditya Muktapida (A.D. 724 - c. 760), a ruler whom the German scholar Hermann Goetz places in the ranks of such great men of history as Alexander, Charlemagne, and Napoleon. Lalitaditya'a reign marks an important turning point in the history of Kashmir: its territorial expansion during his tenure was astonishing. The *Rajatarangini* mentions conquests in India as far as the Deccan, in Afghanistan Tibet, and up to the northern confines of the Central Asian caravan routes at Kucha and Turfan. Lalitaditya's greatest contribution, however, was the impulse he provided in his homeland for the development of all activities, among which those of an artistic and cultural nature occupied a privileged place.

His death, amid the snows of Manchuria, where he is said to have been overwhelmed by enormous enemy forces, was perhaps a historical reality; certainly it is in accord with the myth that grew up around his person.

As so often happens, after the death of Lalitaditya the dynasty languished. The Utpala dynasty that followed was, however, distinguished by two strong and purposeful rulers, Avantivarman (A.D. 856-883) and Sankaravarman (A.D. 883-902). With their passing, however, a slow but inevitable decline set in, both political and cultural, which was to make possible the Muslim conquest of 1339, which the Karkota dynasty in its beginnings had so brilliantly avoided.

The effects of the historical events here summarized are apparent in the various phases of Kashmir architecture. The chronological sequence of the monuments that have come down to us is anything but certain, and scholars—while finding themselves in agreement in attributing a particular group of works to a given historical period—place each monument differently with respect to the supposed line of development of the Kashmir

of works that in some way seem to reflect the serenity enjoyed by the country and the magnificence of the natural environment in which it is immersed.

The history of the "Happy Valley" of Kashmir has its roots in legend, but the folktales related by its people are echoed by a number of respected chroniclers of ancient and recent times. The story of its origin was thought believable even by the Chinese pilgrim Hsüan-tsang, considered by many, because of the prestige he enjoyed, a highly authoritative source. In remote times, say the Kashmiris, their valley was submerged by an immense lake in which a monstrous dragon lived. The good spirits sought to destroy the

soil for no further trace of it is found in the medieval period.

The construction technique differed from the methods employed in neighboring regions, but was simple enough in it use of pebbles mixed with a mortar of mud. Later, in the sixth to seventh century, the pebbles were replaced by larger, unsquared stones, and the interstices thus created were filled with small stones. To obviate the appearance of a surface decidedly disagreeable to the eye, both walls and floors were covered by decorated terra-cotta panels, which were often little masterpieces of applied art. Much as the use of such coverings may produce the impression of a well-developed art, the building techniques of this period were obviously still at a rather archaic level.

It is thus surprising to discover that only a century later local architects were such masters of the technical method of constructing buildings with perfectly square and well-finished blocks, held together by cement mortar or even by the help of metal hooks. This change in building technique was accompanied by an intensification of construction activity. Between the seventh and the tenth centuries the Buddhist complexes of Parihasapura and Pandrenthan were built, as well as the temples at Loduv, Narastan, and Martand, and finally those at Vantipur and Patan, to mention only the most noted.

To what do we owe this exceptional renewal, and what were the stylistic elements that characterized the second phase of Kashmir architecture? Undoubtedly, Lalitaditya's conquests—whose effect was a sudden increase in the national wealth and in the possibilities for more heterogeneous contacts—played an important role. Equally influential was the sovereign's wish to erect monuments that would be both votive offerings to the divinity and tangible signs of his own glory.

The great Karkota ruler, in the course of his expeditions, had seen the monuments adorning the capitals of conquered kingdoms, and certainly many artists must have joined his retinue, bringing with them to Kashmir a rich store of knowledge and experience. The problem is thus one of discerning in the various monuments of the medieval period what has been borrowed and how much is an original contribution by the local culture.

When we compare the Buddhist monuments of Parihasapura and Pandrenthan to those of the previous phase, certain structural changes are discernible. The Cankuna stupa—which takes its name from Lalitaditya's Tocharian prime minister, formerly a functionary at the T'ang court and an intelligent collaborator in the expansionist policy of his king—has a square base and two terraces, with differentiated levels for the ritual circumambulation (*pradaksinapatha*). The chaitya (also at Parihasapura) has now abandoned the apse plan and adopted a square one, even for the inner cell designed to hold the sacred image. The progressive relinquishing of the geometric figure of the circle as a basic structure, in favor of the square, must also have occurred in the sphere of Brahmanic architecture. One notes in fact that the Sankaracarya temple, which may be among the oldest of the

architectural style. We will therefore limit ourselves to a subdivision along general lines (following the criterion already adopted by Percy Brown) and progress through the most significant historical phases.

Local Kashmir tradition would have it that King Asoka himself had gone to the valley and founded the first Buddhist complex on the outskirts of the present Srinagar. But since nothing has been preserved from the Mauryan period, we will consider first that span of time from A.D. 200 to the rise of the Karkota dynasty, which is indeed characterized by monuments inspired by Buddhism. From this first phase of the Kashmir past, only the ruins of Ushkur and Harvan remain today. In these cities, it has been possible to single out a group of buildings connected with the cult: a stupa, a chaitya or sanctuary, a monastery, and other religious structures.

Two highly interesting conclusions can be drawn from a study of the remains at Harvan: the first regarding the structure of the Kashmir stupa in the first centuries of the era under study; the second concerning construction techniques.

The Harvan stupa has not been entirely preserved. All that remains is the base with three successive orders and an access stairway, erected at the center of a quadrangular space. Nevertheless, it is believed that it resembled the numerous images of stupas found on stamped terra-cotta plaques. The dome was thus crushed at the center, and the traditional "umbrellas" of Indian models were replaced by a pyramidal structure with thirteen levels. The chaitya, on the other hand, was closer to the Indian type, preserving the apse plan illustrated so magnificently in India at Karli and Bhaja. It is evident, however, that this plan did not enjoy excessive favor on Kashmir

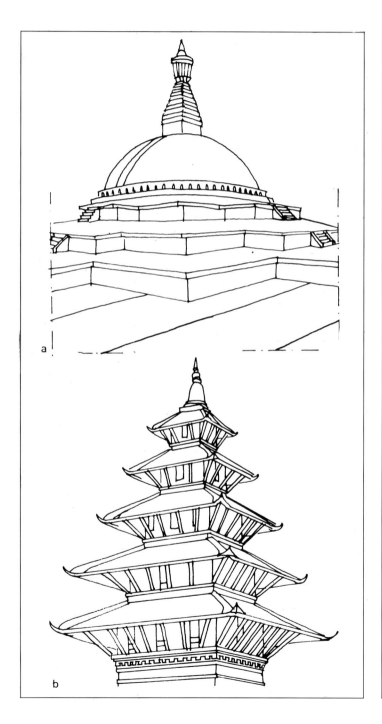

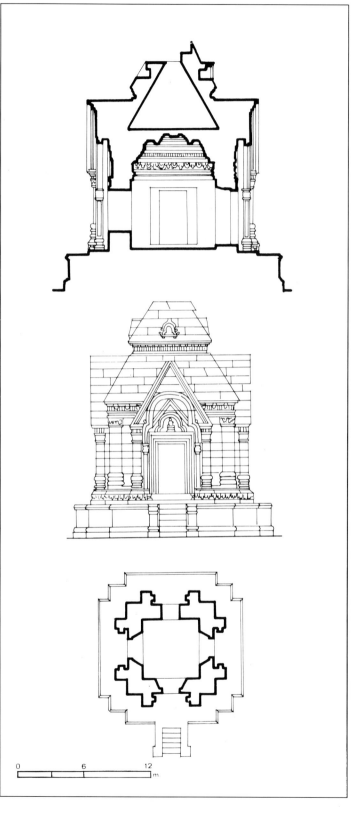

9. *Pandrenthan, temple of Siva Rilhanesvara, section, elevation, and plan* (Enciclopedia Universale dell'Arte).

10. *Pandrenthan, temple of Siva Rilhanesvara.*

Lalitaditya period (though scholars are not in full agreement on this point), is square on the outside and circular within, while later temples are definitely oriented toward the quadrangular form. While it cannot be excluded that some of these modifications should be attributed to changes in ritual, most of them certainly came about for aesthetic reasons.

It has been pointed out that medieval Kashmir architecture took Gandhara architecture as its model, in particular such important Buddhist monuments in the Swat Valley as the Guniyar monastery and the Takht-i-Bahi stupa. It is sufficient to compare the latter with the Temple of the Sun at Martand to be convinced of this. The general arrangement—that is, the open quadrangular space surrounded by chapels—is the same. In the center, the stupa is to one side, and the cell or *garbha griha* to the other. An examination of the individual structures, however, reveals some differences. At Martand, in fact, we already find the three elements that can truly be considered intrinsic to Kashmir architecture: the trilobate arch, the triangular tympanum (sometimes broken), and the pyramidal roof. The first two embellishments were also known to Gandhara artists, and it is to the credit of the Kashmiris that they were able to bring them together in such a way as to form a decorative element of refined taste.

Reduced to such terms, the differences would seem minimal and would serve to support the assertions of those who are convinced of a more or less direct Gandhara derivation. But, apart from the fact that several centuries lie between the two monuments cited—during which time such events as the invasion by the White Huns surely brought about an interruption in cultural exchanges between the two regions—it seems to us that the Temple of the Sun at Martan is of a completely different order from the Takht-i-Bahi stupa.

In fact, both Percy Brown and Hermann Goetz maintain that a Classical derivation is to be seen in Kashmir architecture, not one borrowed through Gandhara, as has hitherto been held, but adopted directly. At this point, however, the positions of the two scholars diverge, with Brown putting the accent on the contribution of Greco-Roman art, and Goetz on that of Syriac-Byzantine art. The second hypothesis is to be preferred, not only for obvious considerations of chronology, but also because Kashmir architecture never achieves Classical levels of harmony and equilibrium. Its Classical elements rest in its technique of construction and use of an "almost Doric" capital, whose presence gave rise to the first doubts about a direct derivation from Ganhara, which favored the Corinthian capital. The Martand temple, in fact, is not free of imbalances and imperfections. The local artists themselves must have been aware of these flaws, for in a later period they were partly eliminated. The Avantisvami temple, for example, is a less imposing but undoubtedly more perfect work. Avantisvami—the temple at Vantipur dedicated to Vishnu—and the Sankaragaurisvara and Sugandhesa temples at Patan represent the moment of perfect equilibrium, the crystallization of the theoretical ideal of Kashmir builders.

The design of the Avantisvami temple is similar to that of Martand, but here an inner and an outer colonnade enrich the sixty chapels surrounding the central courtyard. The outer colonnade runs along the perimeter wall and harmoniously connects the outer façade of the building, which acts as an entrance, with the sacred enclosure (placed slightly to the rear). The central open space of the sanctuary contains a pool for ritual ablutions, and at the corners four small lesser temples.

Later temples—except perhaps for the twelfth-century one of Siva at Pandrenthan, which is characterized by the "lantern" dome typical of Central Asia—wearily repeat the same motifs and remain to attest a process of decadence that becomes progressively more evident up to the moment of the Muslim conquest.

Nepal

The present independent state of Nepal includes a good part of the southern slope of the Himalayas. It is bordered on the north by high mountains and extends southward toward the *tarai*, a plain still largely covered by jungle.

But the heart of Nepal, the area inhabited since antiquity and which until the advent of the Gurkhali dynasty also corresponded to the political confines of the state, is the basin formed by the Bhagmati Valley. Nepal, like Kashmir, was favored on diverse occasions by its geographical position in the pursuit of an isolationist policy that shielded it from the military ambitions of the two colossi pressing against its borders—Tibet and India.

Local tradition relates that Asoka, the "sovereign dear to the gods," was the first illustrious visitor to the land that was the birthplace of Buddha, the Enlightened One: the discovery of a column with an inscription by this ruler in Lumbini Park on the outskirts of Kapilavastu would seem to support this version. Nevertheless, it remains difficult to establish whether Asoka's journey took place solely for devotional reasons, or rather, as seems more

20, 21. *Patan (Nepal), view of Darbar Square.*

likely, these were simply a screen to conceal the king's intention to inspect his distant dominions.

We have no other information on events preceding the rule of the Licchavi dynasty except that concerning the court of the Sakya princes. It was from this line, which had its capital at Kapilavastu—present-day Tiraulakot, where excavations have recently been carried out—that Prince Siddhartha Gautama, called Sakyamuni or Buddha, was born; he spent part of his earthly life nearby (sixth to c. fifth centuries B.C.). The city soon fell into ruin, and the Chinese pilgrims Fa-hsien and Hsüan-tsang, respectively of the fifth and seventh centuries A.D., already found nothing but the foundations of a few houses and a number of holy buildings, stupas, temples, and monasteries. Today, on the supposed site of Buddha's birth, one can see a chapel and the Asoka column that we have already mentioned.

Certain Buddhist monuments on the outskirts of Patan would also seem to belong to the third century B.C., the most notable being the Piprahva stupa and the Chabahil complex, where today it is still possible to admire the great stupa named for Carumati. The legend of Carumati describes her as a daughter of Asoka who settled in Nepal, where she gave considerable encouragement to the religious activity of the region and promoted the construction of numerous holy buildings.

The Chabahil stupa provides a point of departure for describing Nepalese variations on this type of monument, so important in the history of Indian architecture, even if there is some question whether the stupa should not be considered a work of sculpture rather than of architecture. In the beginning, the Nepalese stupa adhered sufficiently to its Indian prototypes. It was dominated by a great hemispherical dome—with chapels at intervals—on which a plinth (*harmikā*) supported the final pyramidal part with its thirteen steps (as a variant we also find thirteen diminishing circles). The *harmikā* is characterized by the presence of an outline of a human face, in which the large painted eyes are especially conspicuous.

These additions are not accidental and correspond precisely to Buddhist symbology; the thirteen levels surely stand for the thirteen heavens, the long path that one must pursue to reach enlightenment. As for the meaning of the painted eyes on the *harmikā*, opinions are not always in agreement. They are generally held to represent the Buddha as "he who sees all," an aspect of the Enlightened One especially felt by the local population, since it had been grafted onto a previous sun cult. There is, however, Volwahsen's suggestive hypothesis, according to which this usage would derive from an exact representation of the stupa as Purusa, the primordial human being. In Indian architecture, in fact, the relation between the structure of the human body and architectural structure is extremely evident and is referred to in the texts. The stupa would thus not be an exception to this rule, and in this case the presence of a human face on the four sides of the plinth can be logically explained.

Thus, with its initial structure remaining fixed, the Nepalese stupa may

22. Bhadgaon, royal palace, detail of a window.

23. Bhadgaon, royal palace, the   ▷
Golden Door.

24. Bhadgaon, Nyatpola Deval,   ▷
temple of Isvari.

25. *Katmandu, temple of Jasamptur,*
detail of the façade.

26. *Spiti Valley, Tabo monastery*
with its eight temples.

27, 28. *Spiti Valley, Tabo monastery,*
view of the temples.

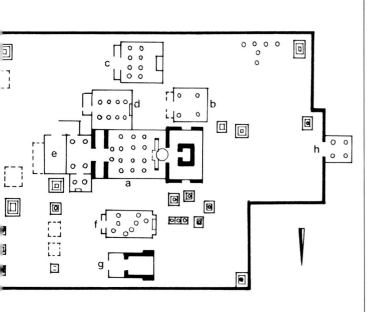

a) gtsung-lag-k'an; b) dkyil-k'an; c) gser-k'an; d) aBrom-ston lha-k'an;
e) sgo-k'an; f) Byams-pa'i lha-k'an; g) aBrom-ston lha-k'an; h) dkar-abyun
(E.U.A.).

articulate itself differently, both in the base and in the cupola. In the Bodhnath stupa, for example, the base is constituted by two large terraces with differentiated levels, while in the so-called Five Stupas in Patan the dome is not perfectly hemispherical; it bulges at the point of juncture with the lower wall, itself curvilinear, which acts as a connecting element between the *anda* (cupola) and the base. Finally, the Svayambhunatha stupa, in addition to the enrichment of its *harmika* by metal and ivory insets, displays four pointed panels placed in such a way as to correspond with the four cardinal points, with sculptured images to the five Dhyani Buddhas.

Nepalese history in the first centuries of our era is marked by the progressive rise of the Licchavis, who must have enjoyed a certain prestige even beyond the national borders, since Chandragupta, the founder of the Gupta Empire in India, asked to marry one of its princesses. Amsuvarman (A.D. 585-650), the founder of the succeeding Thakuri dynasty, was in close contact with the famous Tibetan sovereign Sron-btsan-sgam-po, to whom he had given his daughter in marriage. This Thakuri princess is an important figure in Tibetan history, since some of the credit for spreading Buddhism in court circles has been attributed to her. The fact is all the more significant when one remembers that in Nepal, contrary to what might have been expected, it was Hinduism that prevailed over Buddhism.

The country's political history also indicates the path to follow in singling out major artistic trends; indeed, in the period we will call Licchavi-Thakuri, a strong Indian influence made itself felt, especially in the eastern regions dominated first by the Pala dynasty and later by the Sena. Moreover, we know that during the following century the country passed under Tibetan rule, which was prolonged for a period of time that still cannot be clearly specified. There occurs almost a historical void, an obscure period in Nepalese history lasting virtually until the thirteenth century and yielding only fragmentary and sometimes conflicting information.

Around 1200 a new dynasty, the Malla, rose to power. It was destined to last until 1768, when the country was shattered by the conquering impetus of the Gurkha sovereign Prithvi-Narayan-sah, who founded the dynasty that

30. *Spiti Valley, Tabo monastery, stupa.*
31. *Spiti Valley, Tabo monastery, façade of the Du-vong.*

is still in power. As we see, Nepal remained untouched by the Muslim expansion, and to this distinction it owes the preservation of that predominantly Hindu character, unchanged over the centuries, that still imparts great fascination to the country.

The Malla dynasty encouraged the formation of large urban centers, as is attested by its three great capitals, Katmandu (Kantipur), Patan, and Bhadgaon, erected at a short distance from each other and dominating the communication roads with the interior and with India. These three cities have in common not only their function, but also their arrangement of the principal buildings and quarters. The center of Patan, for example, is constituted by a public square, around which rise the royal residence and the administrative offices. The square, which was used for religious and civil ceremonies, was often embellished by columns with sculptural groups representing rulers or divinities of the Hindu pantheon. It thus became the crossroads, the true center of convergence for all city life. It would therefore be obvious that the streets diverged from it, extending themselves radially to divide the various quarters of the city. This urban structure is extremely interesting sociologically as well, especially when one considers that each quarter was inhabited by a particular social class and all converged toward the Darbar Square almost confusedly, as though the builders' single concern was to maintain the connection with the center.

In any case, the city as a whole is picturesque, as is the individual building. The typical house of the Newaris, the ancient ethnic group that originally dominated the region, is built around an inner courtyard where all domestic activities took place. The building, in brick, generally includes three stories. Each story serves a different function and is therefore articulated in a different way. The façade displays a use of full and empty spaces that—though chiefly dictated by technical requirements—does not lack aesthetic effects. The first story is usually lightened by the presence of a portico that creates an area of shadow, while the second, in its compactness, reflects the light in full. The flat surface is interrupted, however, by the window element, typical of Nepalese architecture and justly renowned for the exquisite delicacy of its execution. The very wide outer frame is worked in wood, with projecting jambs, an upper cornice of considerable dimensions, and a much smaller lower one. A curvilinear fillet, sometimes further embellished by carved figures, may be added to these elements. The window space is filled by a metal grating. Another area of shadow is created at the third story, and is defined by the slope of the roof, supported by a series of richly carved beams.

To conclude the subject of civil architecture, one might say that in Nepal a taste for decoration clearly prevails over structural considerations, and it is the effect of light and plastic form that is chiefly sought. Thus, extreme care is sometimes reserved for details, as can be seen in the windows or the splendid doors of principal buildings such as, for example, the Golden Door of Bhadgaon; or even in constructions created for eminently practical

33. *Buildings in the Tibetan area:
a) Gyantese, the kumbum; b) and
c) Tibetan temple, longitudinal section
and ground plan* (Enciclopedia
Universale dell'Arte).

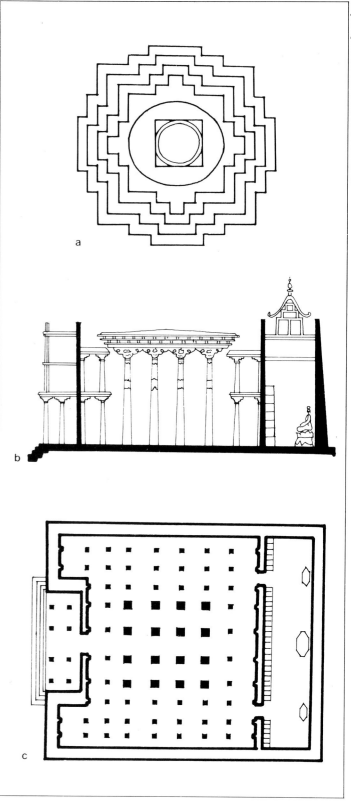

a

b

c

purposes, such as fountains.

Religious architecture clearly complies with different requirements, and is, as always, conditioned by its function. The element common to all temples is the square cell containing the divine image, surrounded by a dense colonnade (which partially hides it from view) and erected on a series of diminishing plinths. One approaches by a staircase flanked by zoomorphic and anthropomorphic figures. The distinguishing element, on the other hand, is the roof, which may be either of the sikhara or pagoda type.

Both of these terms require a word of explanation here. The sikhara roof, borrowed from India, consists of a very accentuated elevation of the upper part following a curvilinear tendency, and probably derives from an ancient roof obtained by the joining of four long rushes laid over a quadrangular structure. The pagoda is the well-known system requiring a series of roofs of decreasing size supported by oblique beams. This type is especially characteristic of Far Eastern regions, but its origin may well have been in India. some Scholars maintain that it is derived from the succession of umbrellas on the stupa; and others, as Percy Brown has shown, from Indian models in the Malabar and Kanara regions. Worthy examples of one and the other type still adorn the sacred buildings of the three capitals. The Nyatpola temple in Patan (built in the first years of the eighteenth century during the reign of Bhupatindramalla) and that of Vatasaladevi in Bhadgaon are two examples.

A study of Nepalese architecture is not complete without mention of the Krishna Mandir temple in Patan. Relatively late and constructed in stone (it should be remembered that the material primarily used here is brick, in the most varied dimensions), it is composed of three spacious superimposed colonnades, enlivened by the presence of chapels that help to impart to it a sense of airiness. It possesses an almost "classical" rhythm that the architecture of the region had never known before.

The Gurkhali architecture of the nineteenth and twentieth centuries, while remaining within the fold of tradition and thus maintaining the archaic atmosphere that pervades the royal cities, often avails itself of the influence of Western architects, particularly French and Italian.

Tibet

Tibet's geographical posititdon as the highest country in the world has often been the inspiration for such poeticisms as the "roof of the world," the "country of snows," and others equally appropriate. Indeed, Tibet is an extended plateau averaging about 16,000 feet and covered with snow for long periods. The country's economy is based essentially on cattle raising, since agriculture is profitable only in the valleys adjacent to the great rivers—the Indus, the Sutlej, and the Brahmaputra. In short, it is a land that offers its inhabitants scant possibilities for survival, one that chiefly lends itself to the nomadic or semi-nomadic life of its shepherds and livestock breeders.

it was followed by the Tibetans for many centuries even after the introduction of Buddhism.

The beginning of the seventh century A.D. brought to Tibet the demise of the existing political order and the rise of the monarchy. This new concentration of power in the hands of a single individual permitted the realization of undertakings (such as national reunification and territorial expansion) that would have been impossible for the extremely divided local potentates. The realities of the situation would indicate that the first two sovereigns, K'ri-slon-brtsan (A.D. 590-620) and Sronbtsan-sgam-po (A.D. 620-649), worked hard to keep the feudal aristocracy under control; the struggle between the monarchy and the local aristocracy, sharpened also by the religious factor, remained one of the salient characteristics of Tibetan history.

Meanwhile, Buddhism had penetrated Tibet with the advent of Sron-btsan-sgam-po's marriages to two princesses, one Nepalese, the other Chinese, who were followers of this faith. Although it was at first limited to the sphere of the court, Buddhism received considerable impetus from another famous ruler, K'ri-sron-lde-brtsan (A.D. 755-797). It was he who declared it the state religion, promoted the creation of monastic centers, and invited the magician Padmasambhava to Tibet. This thaumaturge from the Swat Valley founded the sect of the Red Caps (later to be opposed by the Yellow Caps). K'ri-sron-lde-brtsan's next step was to embark on a wide-ranging expansionist policy abroad, which eventually led to his occupation of Changan, the T'ang capital. With his passing, the monarchy began to decline, and we have only the vaguest information about the period from the middle of the ninth century through all of the tenth. A rebirth—a religious one, but religion and politics are often difficult to distinguish in Tibet—occurred from the eleventh to the twelfth centuries, as a result of missionary work by Atisa, a scholar from the Indian university of Vikramasila, and his disciples. The subsequent Mongol invasion deprived Tibet of its independence and tied its destiny to that of a foreign power, whether of the Mongols themselves or of China proper. In the sixteenth century, the Dalai Lamas created the so-called Lamaistic state, which was to last until the 1950s, when Tibet passed definitely into Chinese hands.

The conclusion that can be drawn from this very brief historical panorama is that life in Tibet hinges on the religious factor. If it is true, as Petech says, that Tibetan chronicles are "stories of the clergy, and biographies are hagiographies," then architecture and the figurative arts are no exception.

Tibetan religious architecture looks principally toward two types of monuments, the chorten and the temple. The chorten derives from the stupa but, compared to its model, involves modifications in structure and function. It has a square base (throne), four steps, and a pot-shaped cupola of modest size, on which is superimposed a pyramidal structure composed of thirteen umbrellas or wheels, then a half-moon, a sun, and a pinnacle. These five elements can be schematized in five geometric figures that correspond to

Obviously, such an economy involves suitable social structures. The archaeological and literary sources are not of much help in reconstructing Tibetan history, but it is not unlikely that the early Tibet of our era was based on a feudal society, the heritage of a more ancient division into territorially settled clans or tribes.

Tibetan religious activity plays an equally important role in the country's history, and to some degree it too has been favored by the Tibetan economy. Primitive Tibetan religion (Bonpo) hinged in fact on shamanistic practices, linked to propitiatory rites involving the magical powers of the celestial and infernal worlds. It was a religion that often went over into superstition, but

36. Yarlung Valley, upper part of a chorten.
37. Yarlung Valley, castle of Yumbulakang (Yum bu bla mk'ar).

the five elements of Vajrayana mysticism, the five mystic syllables, the five colors, and the five mystic parts of the human body.

The chorten (a term that Tucci defines as "a receptacle, a support for offerings") emerges as a funerary monument and as an actual receptacle for sacred objects, placed there at the moment of consecration, or even later by whoever wishes to be rid of them without committing sacrilege (a special opening was left for this purpose). Later, the ritual character was accentuated (the rites necessary for consecration involved circumambulation of the stupa while repeating the phrase *om mani padme hūm*), and finally the chorten acquired a salvational significance.

There are eight types of chorten, and they repeat substantially those of Indian stupas, which take their names from events in Buddha's life. Thus, for example, we have the "great enlightenment" chorten, the "preaching" chorten, the "descent from heaven" chorten, the chorten "of many doors" (or "victorious" chorten), and so forth. The visitor to Tibet can observe along the most frequented routes of the plateau many such structures, connected by low walls on which the words *om mani padme hum* appear. Later changes in the initial pattern involve the chorten's proportions and its base—the latter, in the largest examples (called *sKu-abum*, the hundred thousand images), is articulated in successive planes, designed to contain a series of chapels sheltering various divinities. These divinities change from plane to plane in relation to their greater complexity with respect to the initiatory revelation that will take place at the top. It is thus a pyramid that aims to express the process by which the worshiper is brought from multiplicity to the summit of the One.

The symbology connected with these sacred buildings is extremely complex and is related to the mandalas reproduced on *tankas,* the renowned silk paintings typical of Tibet; however, it is not our task to explore it here. We might simply point out once again the clearly subordinate relationship existing between architectural structure and religious requirements.

The temple, too, shows a development of its own. The archaic type, found primarily in western Tibet, consists of a quadrangular cell with a *pronaos,* or covered veranda. Inside, on the back wall, there was generally a niche to hold the statue of the divinity, and a corridor for circumambulation. One finds, however, even in temples older than the eighth to ninth centuries, more articulated structures. At Samye, a site famous for its monastic complex because of its connection with the figure of Padmasambhava—who may have been summoned to Tibet precisely to exorcise this place—there rises a three-story temple, square in plan, and with four stupas at the sides. Here the height is justified by the cosmic symbolism of the monument, since it is intended to represent the holy mountains and the person of the king, in his quality of Dharmaraja. This notwithstanding, the tendency toward elevation is clear. At Iwang the building is enlarged only by its two side chapels, but at Samada we already find two stories; and, passing through the aforementioned Samye temple and the later Lha K'an at Tholing, we slowly arrive at the nine stories of the Ushando temple. The dimensions of the building also increase proportionately, the atrium becomes wider—at Gyantse it actually functions as a meeting hall for the monks—and the courtyard before the sanctuary is surrounded by a covered veranda with chapels at intervals. The outer façade is distinguished by the veranda, supported by pillars, and by the outer band of the roof, richly decorated with sculptural elements representing animals or particularly significant symbols. In more complex examples, the interior appears as a large hall subdivided into three naves by a double row of columns with painted capitals. The roof is flat and has a central opening; at times the latter is replaced by side openings that run the whole perimeter of the hall between the walls and roof.

The temple constituted the center of monastic activity, but around it rose actual cities in which convents, libraries, and meeting halls eventually took their place.

Civil architecture is rather uniform. The typical house is trapezoidal in form, resting on a somewhat massive stone base, on which walls of sun-dried bricks are built that decrease in thickness and tend to taper toward the top. The roof is always flat. The whole decorative aspect, the pillars adorning the façade, the trapezoidal windows, and the balustrades are of wood, variously painted. Depending on the economic assets of the owner, the building may reach a height of two to three stories or even more; some castles, or dsongs, and royal palaces—such as the Potala, the former residence of the Dalai Lamas in Lhasa, or the palace in Ladakh—are as high as nine stories. The Tibetan fortress departs from the austere and imposing model of the civil building, and adds elements characteristic of military architecture: towers, fortified walls, bastions, and drawbridges.

We may conclude by saying that Tibetan architecture must be considered an artistic activity of minor importance in the country, and therefore one in which external suggestions are accepted without any critical evaluation on the aesthetic level. Thus, it is not unusual to find buildings in which each story follows a different style: Indian, Chinese, Khotanese. One distinction can be made on the basis of function: civil architecture readily indulges a taste for color (the wood of the windows, the red band running along the walls under under the roof) and folklore; while religious architecture accepts the patterns dictated by tradition and turns primarily to Indian models.

In short, architecture in Tibet becomes a noble art when it is charged with symbolic meanings, when it is sacred art, when "to construct" (if we may borrow Tucci's expression) means "to remake the world" by following the pattern of a mandala.

Chiara Silvi Antonini Colucci

Introduction

In our study of the architecture of Central Asia, we will concentrate on the present Soviet Socialist Republics of Turkmenistan, Tadzhikistan, Uzbekistan, and Kirghizia, southern Siberia, and Chinese Turkestan. From proto historical times until our own era, Central Asia has been the theater of countless historical vicissitudes—from the nomadic migrations of the centuries that straddles the beginning of the Christian Era, to Iranian and Chinese domination, and finally to the formation of local empires or of small independent states. These are circumstances that make it extremely difficult for a discussion such as ours to observe criteria of classification based on present geo-political realities. A historical-cultural subdivision that takes into account the structure of Central Asia in more ancient periods will be far more suitable for our purpose. We will therefore divide the territory into western Central Asia, comprising the regions that gravitated politically or culturally toward the empires of the West; and the east-central area, known as Serindia, which, as its name indicates, flowered, culturally speaking, under the influence of India and China. In addition, so many monuments have been brought to light in all the decades of excavation and exploration that we cannot possibly approach our subject from that perspective. To resolve this problem, we will instead set forth the essential lines of the process of urbanization and architectural development, beginning with the most ancient of the Central Asian settlements.

Western Central Asia

For twenty years, Soviet archaeologists have been studying the remains of Focal cultures dating as far back in time as the Neolithic period (fourth to third millennium B.C.). It is now possible to locate the beginnings of these civilizations in time and space, and simultaneously to appreciate the high level of social organization achieved by the earliest groups of sedentary settlers in the region. The first of the two oldest settlements, which was found in southern Turkmenistan, shows important analogies with the organization of contemporary cultures of the Iranian plateau. The second such settlement was discovered in Khwarizm, the region lying between the two tributaries of Lake Aral, the Oxus and the Jaxartes (present-day Amu Darya and Syr Darya), and the protohistorical home of the Kel'teminar culture of the ancient Persian province of Chorasmia. Here we already find the nucleus of the two fundamental types of dwellings, which in modern language might be called "community" and "one-family."

According to an ethnographic definition still valid today, community villages belonging to the Kel'teminar culture are house-villages. We find that they are reduced to a construction, ovoidal in plan and large enough to shelter over one hundred people, with a wooden framework composed of three concentric rows of vertical poles and a series of horizontal beams that support the roof of rushes. The central poles reached a height of 26 to 32 feet, and at the top a circular opening was left for light and air, and

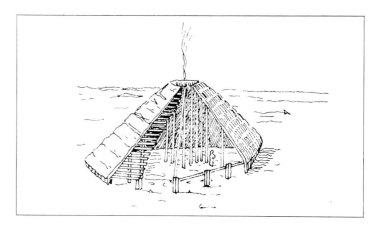

especially to allow the escape of smoke. The numerous hearths inside the house were assigned for domestic use, except for a large hearth about 3 feet in diameter that was presumably of a religious nature. The interior of the house-village was thus divided into two sectors: one for domestic life and the other for community life, the latter centering around the cult of fire.

The other type was undoubtedly more complex and showed a remarkable capacity for urban planning. The village was divided into two sections, western and eastern, separated by a large central artery. Dwellings, formed by a single room sheltering several "families," were placed in the western part; in the eastern section, isolated buildings served a religious and social function in a broad sense. The sites of Akca-tepe, Jalangac-tepe, and Mullali-tepe, all belonging to the Geoksjur culture, are laid out according to this pattern. The last two localities, at a higher level, show an important innovation: a canal-wall, interrupted at intervals by circular spaces, surrounded the entire village.

Archaeological evidence for the second millennium is supplied by Khwarizm, which in these later centuries saw the flowering of the Tazabag'jab and Surjargan cultures. Their settlements show that in the meantime notable changes had occurred such as the use of clay and the introduction of the rectangular house. This progress can no doubt be ascribed to climatic variations and probably also to the advent of a new population that constructed its dwellings in a different way.

In the first half of the first millennium B.C., the Neolithic cultures of Margiana (Jaz-tepe), Bactria (Kobadian), Fergana (Cust), Sogdiana (Afrasiyab), and Khwarizm (Kjuzeli-gyr), all presenting a similar cultural appearance, emerged and developed. The inhabitants of these regions introduced innovations in building techniques that may seem of little importance—among them the use of raw clay bricks—but which in reality were destined to be taken up again, perfected, and to have great significance

39. Collective hut of the
protohistorical culture of Kel'teminar.
Reconstruction on the basis of
archaeological data verified at
Dzanbas-kala (Khwarizm) (from
Tolstov, 1948).

40. Dzanbas-kala, center of the
Kangjuj culture.

in the period immediately following. New needs arose later, for no longer did agriculture wait passively for the earth to produce its crops, but endeavored instead to obtain the maximum yield from its fields. More or less rudimentary canal systems were built, while security for the community was provided by the erection of stockades or defensive walls.

A little later, and almost simultaneously in the various regions of Central Asia, a movement took place that, in accordance with Childe's definition, we may call an "urban revolution"—the birth of true cities. From this moment on, Central Asia was on the road to becoming that "country of a thousand cities" that Classical and Chinese chroniclers recorded in their writings. Fortunately, the work of modern archaeologists is now bringing its kaleidoscopic past to light.

Schematically, we might say that in this period there are two types of cities, the city of inhabited walls and the city of continual construction. Both seem to have had antecedents: the first in the houses of the Amirabad culture (Khwarizm, eighth to seventh centuries B.C.); the second in the protohistorical villages previously mentioned.

The more characteristic model, and one peculiar to Central Asia, was without doubt the city of inhabited walls. As one can easily imagine, it consisted of an enclosing wall built around a quadrangular space left completely free of constructions. The walls, of considerable thickness, were subdivided within into numerous small rooms for use as dwellings, arranged in double or even triple rows; from the outside the walls appeared as actual bastions, reinforced by towers and provided with embrasures. The city was entered by four gates, furnished with a forepart in the form of a labyrinth that constituted a kind of enforced passage. The free space of the interior very likely served to shelter livestock during the night and in the winter months. This type of city is primarily attested in Khwarizm, at Kjuzeli-gyr and Kalaly-gyr (sixth to fourth centuries B.C.), and indeed left a lasting stamp on the region, destined to be reflected in the great defensive structures that characterized the cities and castles of later periods.

Cities of continual construction, on the other hand, took the form of a complex of dwellings grouped in two different sections, sometimes opposite each other and surrounded by the enclosing walls. The type of house it contained might vary from a simple one-room structure to a group of rooms arranged around an inner courtyard. Compared to the plan of previous urban settlements, the structure of these cities showed a notable variation: public buildings (including those for the cult) were grouped inside a fortified citadel—whose function seems to have been quite similar to that of the acropolis in Greek cities—placed at one of the corners of the city.

We must keep in mind that the period in which this exceptional urban development took place corresponds to that of the expansion of the Achaemenid Empire toward the East. There is no doubt that contact with Iranian civilization had profoundly beneficial results for Central Asia. It stimulated cultural enrichment and encouraged trade to a remarkable

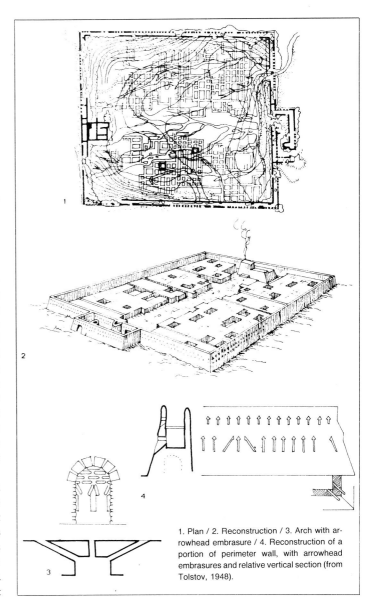

1. Plan / 2. Reconstruction / 3. Arch with arrowhead embrasure / 4. Reconstruction of a portion of perimeter wall, with arrowhead embrasures and relative vertical section (from Tolstov, 1948).

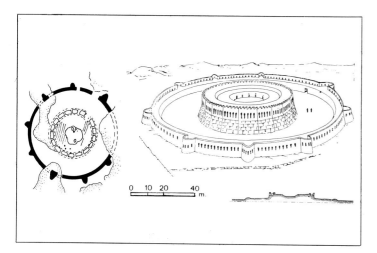

41. *Koj-krylgan-kala, plan and reconstruction of the fortified sacred building (Kangjuj culture), probably a dynastic sanctuary and state center (from Tolstov, 1948).*

degree, thus giving local populations new sources of revenue and contributing in particular to the development of the urbanization phenomenon.

The cities of the sixth to fourth centuries B.C. were vast in extent, with houses that were comfortable and at times even elegant; we note particularly the introduction of columns as supports for the ceilings. There was at that time an unfailing market into which flowed the goods of the West and those of the nomadic East. The material exchange of products was accompanied by meetings and cultural interminglings that in time led to a relatively easy transmigration from one world to another. Different as they were from each other, the peoples of the steppes and of the settled populations nevertheless participated in and profited from this intercommunion.

Bactria, Margiana, Khwarizm, and Sogdiana had in the meantime become territories with an advanced agricultural economy, made possible by a dense and highly efficient network of artificial canals for irrigation, complete with dams. It is precisely this technical perfection and efficiency that has prompted attempts to formulate the hypothesis of a common political structure for the whole western Central Asian area. According to some scholars, a confederation may have emerged of more or less independent states, joined together by a pact of alliance for the maintenance of the canals. Others claim that one of the regions (Khwarizm or Bactria) may have assumed leadership over all the others, imposing a common political order and organizing the distribution of water. Whatever the situation was, it is certain that countless cities flourished during this period. Besides those already mentioned in Khwarizm—to which we can add Dzanbas-kala, Sah-Senem, and Bazar-kala—we might cite Kalaj-mir and Balkh (Bactra) in Bactria, Gjaur-kala in Margiana, Maracanda (the ancient Samarkand) in Sogdiana, and Surabasat in Fergana.

The more southern areas of this territory were successively involved in an event of enormous historical importance: Alexander the Great's victorious march from Greece to India. In reality, from the military and political standpoint, only Bactria can be included among the territories conquered by the Macedonian army, but it is obvious that events of such importance could not have taken place without provoking a whole series of repercussions in the neighboring territories. Moreover, Alexander left behind him armed garrisons, later fortresses; he created cities and erected triumphal arches and altars to the gods—in short, he left tangible traces of his passage. Most of the cities, however, are known to us only from information furnished by his biographers, and modern archaeologists are still striving to retrace this or that city said to have been constructed by him. At the outset of this research, there was little that could be attributed to Alexander and to the period immediately following (during which the so-called Greco-Bactrian kingdom was formed). Such architectural elements as ornamental friezes, columns, and capitals (found in ancient Termez), and some splendid silver coins with the heads of sovereigns, comprised the lot, a paucity that has led to the conviction that the period of the Greco-Bactrian Kingdom had not produced anything in the sphere of plastic and figurative art. Fortunately, the findings of recent years have come to disprove this hypothesis, and today, in addition to Termez, we know of several Greco-Bactrian cities along the banks of the Oxus: Dal'verzin, Kej-kobad-sah, Kuhna-kala, and Ai-Khanum, newer sites that have yielded more or less recognizable vestiges of urban settlements.

Much of the work is still in progress and the data in the process of being interpreted. It is obvious, however, that the Greco-Bactrian city was composed of one-story houses, divided into two principal quarters by a wide street, and characterized by an acropolis and thick defensive walls. In practice, it was extraordinarily similar to cities of the continual-construction type.

There is considerable discussion of the genesis of this urban structure in Central Asia, namely whether it should be considered the natural development of the agricultural villages in the Geoksjur oases of Namazza-tepe or, still farther west, of the lower strata of Anau. It may, on the other hand, have been determined by the Hellenic example that was brought onto Central Asian soil by the first Greeks to arrive there, colonists and war prisoners whom the Achaemenids thought it safer to transport to the eastern regions of their empire. We will restrict ourselves to tangibles and consider only such decorative elements as the stucco moldings, of which remarkable fragments have survived, and the Corinthian capitals long imitated by local artists as being of clear Classical derivation in architecture.

Other important centers thrived outside Bactria. Afrasiyab in Sogdiana, of which the architectural particulars are still not known, must certainly have been a large city, and the site of Koj-krylgan-kala in Khwarizm bespeaks a city so unusual that it deserves to be examined in detail. Koj-krylgan-kala

42. *Ajaz-kala, Chorasmian culture of Kushan derivation. 1. Drawing with a general view of the complex / 2. Architectural details: vertical section of passageway and arrowhead opening (from Tolstov, 1948).*

43. *Toprak-kala, reconstruction of the large castle with three towers, official residence of the Khwarizm rulers (from Tolstov, 1948).*

emerged in the fourth century B.C., in the period that Tolstov calls Kangjuj (an approximate transliteration of the name given to Sogdiana in the Chinese sources), and survived until the fourth century A.D. It shows two successive phases: from the fourth century B.C. to the first century A.D., and from the first to the fourth century A.D. The peculiarities of this locality are essentially two: first, its circular plan, and second, the simultaneous function of the monument as a tomb and as an astronomical observatory. As for the plan, it has been observed that cities with a circular plan are attested among the Assyrians, the Medes, and the Parthians, and from this the logical conclusion has been drawn that the builders of Koj-krylgan-kala were inspired by Western models. It cannot be overlooked, however, that the form of the construction is related to the function of the monument itself, which, though surely built for cult purposes, was also utilized as an observatory. It is thus possible that the origin of this plan was inspired by a precise reason, one to be sought in the sphere of astral-funerary symbology.

Koj-krylgan-kala, in its latter phase, appears as a large construction, 286 feet in diameter, and consists of a central two-story edifice and fortified defensive walls with eight towers and a monumental entrance gate, facing east. The complex is surrounded on the outside by a rampart that is 49 feet wide and 10 feet deep. Originally, the space between the central building and the walls had been conceived as an open courtyard. Later, it was used for the construction of dwellings intended to house persons attached to the cult and engaged in the observation of the stars. Finally, little by little, its defensive character was emphasized—the bastions were reinforced, and embrasures appeared on the outer side of the walls and rampart. Here we can already glimpse the transition, soon to be observed on a broad scale, from the fortified city to the fortress-castle of post-Kushan times.

From the first century B.C. to the sixth century A.D., this area was in fact subject, directly or indirectly, to the Kushan Empire, which was so important to the history of India. The Kushan presence in Central Asia assumed a significance that went well beyond the limits of mere political domination. To be part of this empire meant in effect to be connected with a military strong state, one whose international relations placed it simultaneously in contact with Han China and imperial Rome. It included the benefits of a very extensive trade network, and finally, an exposure to the early teachings of a new creed, Buddhism, which the Kushan rulers had welcomed and were prepared to spread over all the territory they governed. In short, the cultural atmosphere of the Kushan Empire was of the greatest possible breadth, merging as it did the artistic and ideological influences of various fully developed civilizations.

The Kushan period in Central Asia is usually subdivided into "ancient" and "late," in order to make the distinction between two substantially different phases. The first is represented in Bactria, where the Kushan clan began to emerge, coin money, and erect monuments that were already an expression of its sovereignty. Halcajan, the oldest Kushan locality so far

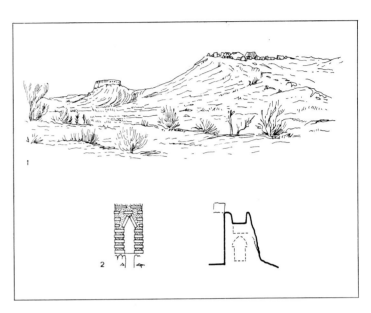

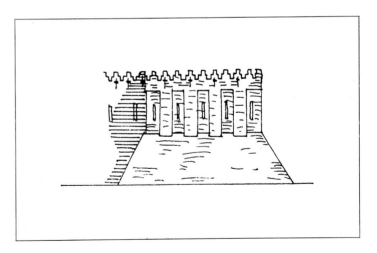

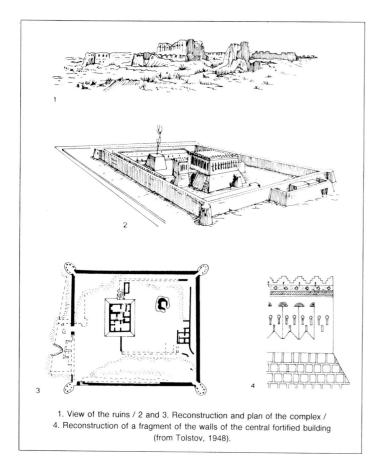

1. View of the ruins / 2 and 3. Reconstruction and plan of the complex /
4. Reconstruction of a fragment of the walls of the central fortified building
(from Tolstov, 1948).

civilization in the first period of its empire, when the Arsacid rulers succumbed to the fascination of Hellenism, is reflected in the great quantity of objects of exquisite taste found in the city of Nisa. Nisa emerged as the principal center of the small Parthian kingdom in the middle of the third century B.C., but, with the growth of the dynasty, it progressively increased in importance and size. The city is divided into two parts, old and new. The first is probably an imperial city and includes fortified castles, temples, and a necropolis for dead sovereigns. Two buildings seem to have had a particular significance: the Square Hall, a room adorned with numerous columns with capitals of the Doric, Corinthian, and Iranian kind, where presumably ceremonies connected with the cult of the dynasty were performed; and the Round Hall, also decorated with columns, which in all probability served as a temple.

The new Nisa substantially represents the true city (going back to the first century B.C.) and includes a fortress, temples with columns, an acropolis, and numerous dwellings. The thick walls of pounded earth covered with brick that surrounded the city had reinforcement towers that today have been largely lost.

Khwarizm has a history of its own within the context of these regions, in that it almost always remained independent or at least autonomous from foreign empires. Nevertheless, both for convenience in classification—and because, as we said, the Kushan presence was a determining one for the whole Central Asian territory—here, too, the period following the expansion of Kangjuj culture is called Kushan. Besides Koj-krylgan-kala, such important centers as the city of Toprak-kala, as well as the fortresses of Kavat-kala, Anga-kala, and Ajaz-kala all belong to it.

Fortress-cities may be said to follow the tradition of the "cities of inhabited walls," in that they appear as isolated complexes with one outer and one inner enclosure wall. In the intermediate space, small separate rooms were built, the so-called dwelling-corridors. The plan is usually quadrangular, and the difference between one fortress and another is reduced to the greater or lesser perfection with which the defensive bastions are constructed. Thus, the one that seems to be the oldest of all, Ata-tjurk-kala, has walls of unbaked bricks and is totally devoid of towers; Kurgasin-kala, on the other hand, has rectangular towers, placed without order and at irregular intervals. A new development appears, however, at Ajaz-kala and Anga-kala: the towers, semicircular or square, are disposed systematically along the walls. It should be noted that these fortresses constituted the centers of agricultural complexes that extended all around them. Here the peasants lived and attended to the work of the fields, having recourse to the protection of the fortress—where an armed garrison was permanently established—only in case of danger.

Toprak-kala, as we have indicated, was a true city and falls within the previous vein of urban tradition, consisting as it did of a citadel, the fortified residence of the local rulers, and of an inhabited center, symmetrically

discovered, is located on the banks of the Surkandarya and dates as far back as the first half of the first century A.D. The most important edifice of the site is the royal palace, rectangular in plan, and including a richly decorated throne room and various other rooms connected by corridors. The architectural layout of the building seems to be of Iranian derivation, as is suggested by the hexastyle iwan and other lesser elements that correspond exactly to those at Surkh Kotal, the city within whose acropolis a temple has been found dedicated to Mithra by the Kushan emperor Kanishka. In both localities, however, the Iranian element has, broadly speaking (we find some components properly belonging to Kushan culture), been overlaid by the Hellenistic one, clearly distinguishable in the decoration.

At the same time the Kushans ruled in Central Asia, the Parthian Empire thrived in the territories of Parthia and Margiana. The splendor of Parthian

V. *Bhadgaon, royal palace in
Darbar Square.*

45. *Yakke-Parsan, reconstruction of Afrigidian center (from Tolstov, 1948).*

46. *Kafyr-kala, vertical section of the rock-cut cupola, covered in stone and bricks. Note the wells for the transition from the square plan of the base to the round one of the cupola (from Litvinsky-Zeimal, 1971).*

divided into two parts by an artery about 26 feet in width. The city was entered through a labyrinth-gate, itself amply attested by tradition. The whole city was enclosed by walls furnished with embrasures and fortified by numerous towers.

It would be worthwhile at this point to examine briefly the different types of embrasures to be found on the outer walls of the city during various periods. In the ancient period—at Dzanbas-kala, for example—they are arranged in two continuous rows, interrupted at regular intervals by a group of three, of which the two side ones are placed obliquely. With the development of supporting towers, the use of triple embrasures is abandoned; the walls become animated and the alternating rhythm between full and empty spaces is emphasized by the introduction of projecting pilaster-strips. Embrasures are then employed on the rear part. Still later, the embrasures are transferred to the pilaster-strips and grouped almost to form a decorative motif. In addition to the arrangement of this important element of defense, it is also worth noting the form of embrasure employed in Central Asia: it is called an arrowhead embrasure from the particular shape of its outline.

To return to Toprak-kala, we may add that its fortification was completed by a moat encircling the outside along the entire arc of the walls. The citadel consisted of three towers placed in the northwest corner, and a royal palace that included a deputation hall, rooms for the sovereign and his harem, inner courtyards, an armory, and above all a fire temple standing directly before the entrance gate of the citadel. Adjoining the acropolis, and thus in the northeast corner, there was a broad open area that in all probability contained the market; then came the twelve residential quarters (six on each side), each of them composed of a certain number of one-room houses, sometimes arranged around an inner courtyard.

Fortunately, Toprak-kala, the royal residence and as such certainly the most important city of the period, has been only partially damaged by time. Not only has it been easy to distinguish its plan, but it has also been possible to recover fragments of the mural paintings that adorned the halls of its buildings, as well as other findings of considerable merit. The cities of Eres-kala, Kyrk-kyz-kala, and Kurganci-kala, which have come down to us in a much worse state of preservation, must have been quite similar.

The archaeological findings for cities emerging in this period in other Central Asian regions are still far from numerous, or at least are not such as to merit particular attention. Tali-Barzu, for example, a city in Sogdiana a short distance from Samarkand, founded around the second or third century of our era, is reduced to a few dwellings and the remains of fortifications.

With the advent of the fourth century, the decline and subsequent fall of the Kushan Empire created a power vacuum in Central Asia, and led to the formation of two different but parallel phenomena: on one side, there existed a consolidation of the supremacy of local lords, who from their castle

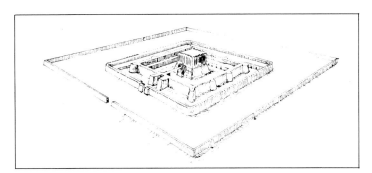

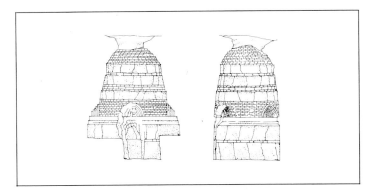

strongholds ruled over the surrounding territory and supervised the regular functioning of the irrigation canals; on the other, there arose a succession of new migrations by peoples from the East, who were attracted to this vacuum and tried to fill it, though in many areas their rule was nominal at best.

In the fifth century the Hephthalites, considered by Buddhist sources (which perhaps exaggerate their ferocity) a true calamity, overran Sogdiana and Bactria in the course of a relentless march to the south. Later, it was the turn of the Turks (T'u-chüeh), who, being much less barbarous than their predecessors, were open to many of the influences that the local culture was prepared to give them. Finally, the Muslim conquest produced a clear break with the past and brought Central Asia within the sphere of a civilization based on entirely different presuppositions. Added to all this was the interference in the area by the two great powers pressing on its confines: to the east, T'ang China, and to the west, Sassanid Iran. The latter had long considered these territories an integral part of its sphere of influence.

Clearly, the historical circumstances were hardly conducive to the existence of large urban agglomerates, and in effect what we see in the fifth

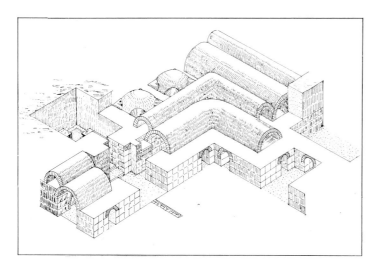

47. Adzina-tepe, axonometric reconstruction of a complex with vaults and domes (from Litvinsky-Zeimal, 1971).

century is a progressive decline of cities. On the one hand, they would have been too easily subject to pillage and destruction, and on the other, there would seem to have been less reason for their existence; in such tormented and insecure times, commercial activity was reduced and an agricultural economy once again prevailed. Thus began the so-called medieval period, which saw the emergence of a feudal society. The process that led to feudalism is quite clear: the agricultural districts, which, as we have previously seen, were already protected by a fortified construction, were transformed into fiefs. The fortified construction thus became a fortress-castle for the local lord and his retinue. The power of the feudatory was in direct proportion to his capacity or possibility for providing prosperity to the agricultural community, and in the final analysis was closely tied to the success of natural or artificial irrigation.

The castle generally show an identical structure. At the center there was a quadrangular tower on a high stylobate or artificial podium; there follows a first enclosing wall, reinforced by semicircular towers, within which runs a continuous series of rooms for habitation. A second enclosing wall is very similar to the first except that it has no towers; a third wall is placed at some distance from the other two. The castle and the first ring of walls were inhabited by the lord and his family, the second by his servants. The space between the second and third circle of walls, left free of constructions, was reserved for agricultural activities useful to the whole community. The only possible variations in this type of plan was one whereby the central edifice was shifted toward the walls or to one corner of the fortress. The subdivision of the castle-tower's inner space assigned for habitation nevertheless undergoes various changes with the passage of time. In an early period the

dwelling rooms take the form of long narrow corridors, with a single opening on the side of the outer wall (as in the Mount Mug castle in Sogdiana); then these same corridors are provided with a central opening, to be transformed little by little into a passageway of greater or lesser width. Moreover, the corridors were also widened, becoming actual rooms that, disposed along the outer wall, served for the various members of the family. At Yakke-Parsan, for example, a space was left free at the center, assuming an importance, as the focal point of the building, that was subsequently emphasized by a domed roof. A further development is shown by the castles of Aktepe in the Tashkent district (with two levels), of Kyrk-kyz (Termez), and Akyrtas (Semirec'e), of the sixth to seventh centuries A.D. Here the proportions are considerably increased, and the building would seem to have been divided into four distinct parts which separate entrances; the parts are connected by corridors and galleries converging toward a central space, either the domed room previously mentioned or an inner courtyard to which everyone had access.

According to the earliest Arab sources, castles numbered in the hundreds. We have tried to indicate their general characteristics, as drawn from the more or less recent findings of the Soviet archaeologists in numerous localities: Tesik-kala, Berkut-kala, Kum Baskan-kala, Yakke-Parsan, and Tok-kala in Khwarizm, Kala-i-Bolo in Fergana, Kalai Mug and Batyr-tepe in Sogdiana, Zang-tepe and Chairabad-tepe in Bactria, and others. Numerous as they were, these castles were clearly not all of equal importance. Gradually, as they grew and developed, the complexes that were favored by their situation along the more frequented trade routes once again assumed their role as cities. They were joined in this transformation by those cities that held positions of particular political and administrative importance either as seats of local justice or because they were in direct contact with the capital of the state to which they belonged.

The names of the cities of this period sound much more familiar, since often they were centers that continued to live and prosper even after the Arab conquest—Samarkand, Bukhara, Merv, for example. Thus, it will not be to these that we will turn in order to describe the typical city of the seventh to eighth centuries, but rather to those cities that soon ceased to exist and that therefore convey an exact image of both the building techniques and the urbanistic conceptions of the period. We find that the Central Asian city of the seventh and eighth centuries is divided into two distinct parts: the citadel and the *sahristān* (the actual city). A ring of walls generally surrounded both, but whereas previously, as construction of the castle proceeded, all vital urban activities were concentrated in its interior, if not actually within the fortress-tower, now little by little political and social life passed beyond the walls of the citadel and were transferred to the *sahristān*. In the space reserved for the latter, temples and administrative buildings were constructed, and here economic and cultural life took place. Two main arteries passed through the complex, connecting the four entrance gates.

48. Adzina-tepe, arch with keystones of cut bricks (from Litvinsky-Zeimal, 1971).

49. Adzina-tepe, plan and elevation (partial) of the so-called northeast façade of the miniature stupa in Room XXXI (from Litvinsky-Zeimal, 1971).

The position of the citadel was not fixed; it might occupy a corner, or be at the center, or even lie outside the walls (as in the case of Isfidzab-Sajram). The two principal streets were usually perpendicular to each other, and the building for the cult was often erected at the point where they met.

Widespread as this pattern was, it was nevertheless not the only one adopted. As we have observed, some of the buildings that should have formed part of the complex enclosed by the walls—the citadel, the temple, or the market, for example—might be placed outside. The plan itself of the whole might vary. If it departed from a more or less quadrangular shape—as at Merv, Hiva, Termez, and Isfidzab-Sajram—it was possible to arrive at that of Balkh, formed by ten wall segments of varying length, or at asymmetrical plans that would actually be difficult to define by any precise geometrical term. The regions of western Central Asia were rich in centers of this type, and it would be pointless to supply the reader with a lengthy list of them. Instead, we will note some particulars of a city that, while certainly not the largest or richest of its time, offers us the inestimable advantage of being archaeologically better documented: Pjandzikent in Sodgiana.

The plan of this city does not depart from the usual pattern. Inside its high walls, which were reinforced by ten oval towers built of unbaked bricks, were the citadel and the *sahristān*. Houses in the latter were distinguished from each other according to the degree of culture, importance, or wealth of the owner. The most magnificent were of vast size, with two stories, and included a reception hall with walls adorned by painting and sculpture, benches of pounded earth that ran along the walls, and a staircase ascending to the upper story. There might also be special rooms devoted to the cult or to cultural manifestations (perhaps theatrical and dance spectacles). Outside, extreme care was lavished on the façades, which were provided with an arcade or a loggia. The roof system might be of the vault, cupola, or lantern type. In the latter, characteristic of the Central Asian area and frequently adopted by local architects, the vault was closed by means of a structure of wooden beams arranged in squares that progressively diminish in perimeter. These squares follow each other symmetrically in such a way that the corners of the higher square are diagonal to the sides of the one beneath. The preferred construction materials were unbaked bricks (measuring approximately $20 \times 10 \times 5$ inches) and wood. Two temples have also been found at Pjandzikent, consisting of a central hall, its roof supported by columns, two side rooms, a courtyard to the east, and a cell (with no communication to the outside) to the west. Around this central structure there were other rooms, assigned to various uses.

So far we have often spoken of cult buildings, but we have not paused to consider one very important sector in the sphere of Central Asian architecture, that of Buddhist edifices and religious architecture in general. It was in the Kushan period that Buddhist architecture evidently emerged, with the spread of this creed beyond the confines of its country of origin.

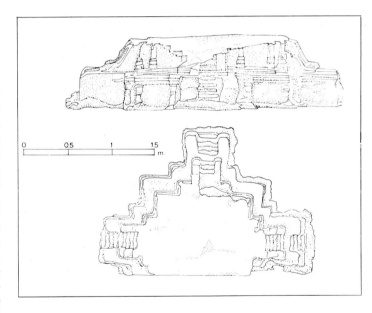

This period also saw the flowering, in India, of the Gandhara school of art, which produced works of great merit by expressing the values of Buddhist thought through forms inspired by the Classical world. This definition is surely simplistic and inadequate, and indicates only two components of the school in question, but it would be inappropriate here to go into the controversial subject of Gandhara art. We have mentioned it only because all scholars agree that the religious painting, sculpture, and architecture of Central Asia have each felt its influence to some degree.

At Kara-tepe, a Buddhist complex carved out of the rock (second to fourth centuries A.D.), the Gandhara influence is obvious, but only in the fragments of sculpture and in the stuccowork, since this type of rock-cut construction goes back to Indian examples that precede the flowering of the artistic school of the northwest. Closer to the Gandhara model—albeit modified by substantial Iranian elements—would seem to be the monasteries and sanctuaries of Bamiyan (northern Afghanistan), a very active Buddhist center of the fourth to seventh centuries A.D. Though the site is famous chiefly because of its mural paintings and its two colossal rock-cut statues of Buddha, some architectural elements are worthy of note, such as the domes of the square-plan caves, and the lantern roof previously mentioned.

Finally, Central Asian monasteries and stupas of the seventh to eighth centuries show that they had assimilated not only the Gadhara example, but also those of Gupta Indian and Sassanid Iran, and above all were able to rework these suggestions in keeping with their own designs. Two localities dating from this period have recently been brought to light: Ak-Besim and Adzina-tepe. The first site has revealed two important Buddhist sanctuaries—one rectangular in plan, the other square—as well as a Nestorian church with a cruciform plan; the second site has yielded a vast sacred area divided into two square adjoining and communicating courtyards within which numerous temples and stupas were constructed.

These findings in the Ak-Besim and Adzina-tepe complexes testify to the full vigor of Buddhism in the late period, while their coexistence with religious buildings pertaining to Zoroastrianism, Manichaeanism, and Nestorianism would indicate a climate of broad tolerance or even of religious syncretism.

Serindia
The link between China and the western regions had been made possible since antiquity by the formation of commercial centers near the oases at the foot of the T'ien-Shan Mountains and along the waterways that supplied the Tarim Basin. Through them passed the great "silk route" used by the Chinese merchants to transport their precious commodity to the West. The caravans, however, not only conveyed Chinese merchandise to India and Iran, and across them to the eastern Mediterranean, but received in exchange products that were distributed throughout their own domestic market. Exchanges took place that only the temporary incursions of nomads

from the steppes (always attracted by the material well-being of the settled populations and eager for plunder) were able to disrupt.

The silk route thus attracted the attention of all the empires that were formed in the adjoining regions, from the Kushans of India to Han China, from the Arabs to the Turks, from the Hsiung-nu to the Hephthalites. The rulers were interested, however, in conquering the territory without jeopardizing the specific function of the city-states—they had no desire to interrupt the flow of trade—and limited themselves to controlling and exploiting these sources of revenue. The centers along the caravan route, on the other hand, were small autonomous entities having no practical possibility for making common cause against the invader; they were instead easy objects of conquest. The desert separated one from another, ensuring that each developed in accordance with its own particular nature, more often in conflict than in union with the neighboring cities. At most it was a question of cities joined more by their capacity to receive foreign influences than by reciprocal exchanges.

The silk route set out from the city of Kashgar, into which flowed the caravans coming from the West, and proceeded along two different paths: a northern one passing through the cities of Tumshuq, Kucha, Shorchuq, Qarasahr, and Turfan; and a southern one that went through Yarkand, Khotan (or Yotkan), Niya, and Miran to link up with the other at Tunhwang on the Chinese border. The first information we have on the city-states of Central Asia appears in Chinese sources of the Han period, and allows us to trace their existence back to the second century A.D. Another highly important source for the history of these cities consists of the travel diaries of Buddhist monks who went on pilgrimage from China to India across the deserts and oases of Central Asia. They accurately described the chief characteristics of the kingdoms they encountered—their climate, agricultural and craft production, customs and costumes, and—naturally—religious institutions, with particular reference to Buddhism. For example, Hsüan-tsang, the most famous of Chinese pilgrims, was able to observe and thus report on many monasteries that in the seventh century were in full activity in Kucha, Aqsu, Karghalik (south of which a large mountain contained a "multitude" of cells and niches for monks), and Khotan. When we remember that by that time no few historical vicissitudes had already disturbed the tranquillity of the Central Asian oases, it is logical to suppose that there had been in previous centuries an even greater number of Buddhist monuments.

The commercial contacts to which we have referred help us also to single out those cultural areas that influenced the artistic development of the various centers and the evolution of thought, transmitting not only figurative models to be reproduced, but above all such religious experiences as Buddhism, Zoroastrianism, Manichaeanism, and Nestorianism.

The sands of the desert, wind, erosion by water, and the hand of man have caused irreparable damage to the structure of these cities, and only

VIII. *Changan (Sian, Shensi),*
pagoda-tomb of Husan-Toang,
T'ang dynasty.

the patient work of such illustrious scholars as Stein, Grünwedel, Von Le Coq, and Oldenburg has made it possible for some part of the art treasures they contained to come down to us. Stupas, monasteries, fortresses, and especially wall paintings and stuccowork remain to testify to a high level of civilization. As for architecture, we can explain its essential substitutive elements, in both the religious and civil spheres, by deducing them from the few surviving monuments that still preserve visible traces of their original structure.

Buddhist architecture can be divided into two large groups: cave temples and open-air constructions. The origin of the cave temple or monastery is undoubtedly Indian, and is connected with the desire of architects of that country to abandon wood as a construction material in favor of something more durable. A natural cave offers the possibility of achieving this purpose, and the enormous patience of the Indian *silpin* smooths the walls, models the vault, and carves all the figurative elements necessary for the cult. But in Central Asia, in most cases, the geological situation is quite different. The rock does not have the granitic consistency of that in India; on the contrary, it crumbles easily, lends itself poorly to the stonecutter's chisel, and may often collapse. In addition, the Central Asian area is frequently subject to seismic disturbances. Given therefore a desire to reproduce Indian models, the cave monasteries of Central Asia were necessarily more modest. We can distinguish four types of caves according to the kind of roof adopted. The first type includes two rooms and a vestibule, and has a ridge vault or a cupola; the second generally adopts only the cupola; and in the third type, the ceilings have false incorbelled beams. Finally, there is a simpler roof system that provides a flat roof with fluting, in imitation of the wooden beams used for houses.

Open-air constructions have obviously survived to a much lesser degree, and often nothing has been found but the remains of foundations. The two most frequent types of monuments are, however, as in all the Buddhist world, the *vihara* or monastery and the stupa. One of the oldest centers from which conspicuous building ruins remain is Miran, where there stood a monastery within which a cell with a domed ceiling held a large stupa. The complex, like that of Ravaq in the Khotan oasis, has been shown to relate to Gandhara prototypes; and while in the case of Miran the relationship is confirmed by an examination of the paintings, which clearly show the influence of the Indian School, at Ravaq the composition itself recalls the monuments of Gandhara. The *vihara* in the Khotanese city contained a stupa, protected by a wall built in a square around it and adorned inside and out by stucco statues of considerable size. The wall is reinforced at the corners; the stupa, cruciform in plan, was erected on a base with three steps.

Unfortunately, the scarcity of archaeological evidence does not even allow us to determine a precise line of development for the stupa. We can only say that the base seems to assume an increasingly important role, with two or three steps (as in the stupas of Endere, Niya, and Ravaq); the cupola either becomes thinner by elongation and replaces the classic umbrellas with a series of superimposed diminishing planes (as in the case of Miran), or is reduced to a very modest size. In general, there is a tendency toward elongation and a vertical development for the whole monument.

As for civil architecture and city planning in general, we have very little to go on. A few beams still fixed in the soil have led to the supposition that houses and palaces in the city-states were composed of a wooden framework and walls of pounded earth that have not withstood the particular climatic conditions of the region. This is too little to give us an idea of what the caravan cities must really have been like, though we know them to have been rich and to have provided a stimulus for every kind of cultural activity. In a few cases, literary and artistic evidence makes up for the archaeological gaps. Thus, since Chinese sources extol the ability of musicians and dancers from Kucha and Khotan, we must suppose that these arts enjoyed great favor in the two cities, and that the artists had at their disposal buildings especially constructed for this kind of spectacle. Similarly, the stories of pilgrims or certain details of frescoes introduce us to the interiors of the royal palaces, whose splendor we can imagine.

Naturally, the cities also provided for constructions of a military nature—bastions, fortifications, and ramparts. It was necessary to prepare a system of defense in order to avoid eventual surprise attacks. As we have seen, however, the inhabitants of the oases were more inclined to peaceful activities than to martial exploits, and for this reason the models for their fortifications were probably borrowed from peoples thought to be more expert in this field. It is not surprising that the forts of Endere and Miran (seventh to eighth centuries) respectively show a clear T'ang Chinese and a Tibetan stamp.

Because of our lack of data, the total picture we have sketched is far from being exhaustive, but it is encouraging to know that archaeologists are persistently continuing their work of extracting from the desert any slight trace of the past. Perhaps someday soon the physical appearance of the ancient cities of the silk route can be more fully reconstructed.

Chiara Silvi Antonini Colucci

Chinese architecture, it is often said, contains no clear stylistic differences, but only a slow evolution from simple to more complex forms. This opinion can be attributed to the predominantly wooden nature of the buildings—a technique ill suited to revolutionary developments; and to the establishment since earliest times of certain essential characteristics for the most widespread type of building—the pavilion (*tien*), with its tripartite structure consisting of the base (*chieh-chi*), the columns (*chu*) that support the system of corbels (*tou-kung*), and the roof covering (which immediately takes on an overriding importance in the structural harmony of the whole building). All of these factors lend credence to this idea. At the same time the complicated geomantic, ritual, and sumptuary regulations that link all new constructions with a past viewed as perfect in the Confucian sense would seem to confirm the common impression.

Even the way in which the buildings are laid out is typical and does not seem to change much through the centuries. The monumental conception of a building complex, seen only in the horizontal sense—that is, with broad but not especially high structures, placed in an orderly fashion in accordance with a particular rule of proportion by which no element can exist apart but is completed by a similar and opposite one—goes directly back to the Chou dynasty.

These basic characteristics, together with a love for nature and the desire not to disturb it by works that might upset its balance—interference that would have grave consequences on the magical level—form part of Chinese humanism and are prompted by the socio-political and religious forces that help to shape it.

Actually, Confucian pragmatism is directly responsible for the rigid standard of axiality and symmetry that made it possible to arrive at a graduated and hierarchical order in the city. The royal palace was placed at the center of the urban system: the network of streets, the dwellings, the directional complexes, and the service areas. This hierarchical process is also found in the countless sumptuary regulations that determine colors, materials, installations, and the structures of dwellings in relation to every step in the social ladder.

The other aspects of Chinese religion (and philosophy), Taoism, is instead responsible for the ecological sensibility by which Chinese architecture is related to nature and the surroundings: walls follow the contours of hills, even so colossal a work as the Great Wall, and splendid imperial gardens include lakes, rivers, and hills. If, as is often the case, these elements are artificial, they are nevertheless carried out with wonderful naturalness. The rocks, pebbles, and plants in small gardens, though laid out in accordance with mysterious rhythms and well-defined magical relationships, give the marvelous impression of having been put there by the whim of Nature, even when they are simply the fruit of a refined sensibility. These architectonic poetics, applied but neither codified nor recognized—since architecture has never been a true art for the Chinese and thus, aside from

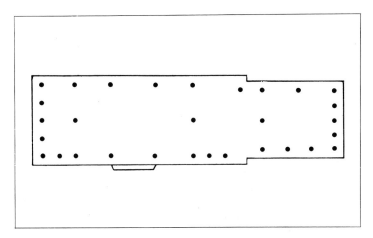

52. *Anyang (Honan), plan of a large rectangular building, Shang dynasty (from Sick-man-Soper, 1956).*

53. *Wu-Kuan Ts'un (Honan), aerial view of a large Shang dynasty tomb.*

a few technical construction manuals, there are no adequate treatises on the subject—would seem to be extremely valid, given their successful diffusion throughout the Far East, which began in the Han period and was later extended.

The interest aroused by modern Japanese architecture among artists and critics all over the world confirms this validity, since many poetic canons of ancient China still underlie, in re-elaborated forms, the works of the best contemporary masters.

It is precisely this undoubted validity and its consequent duration over the centuries that have suggested the idea that Chinese architecture is totally lacking in stylistic variations. Only our Western taste prevents us from noticing at first sight the profound differences between a T'ang building and a Liao building, so bedazzled are we by the exoticism of these works and ill prepared to grasp their cultural foundation and variations.

To demonstrate that constant innovation, changes in style, and revivals exist in the development of Chinese architecture, we will try to adopt, in this very different field, the nomenclature employed in the West to describe the progress of our own architecture.

It is an ambitious attempt, which errs first of all by the rigidity and arbitrariness inherent in any system of classification. On the other hand, since architecture is singularly linked to the social factor that directly gives rise to it, it may seem impossible to employ correctly terms conceived to define phenomena that have manifested themselves in a completely different world. Nor would this seem suitable for the purpose of clarifying a stylistic evolution that, whatever our sentimental esteem for it, is in a certain sense alien to our way of considering architecture. Nevertheless, it is my belief that correspondences exist (almost undefinable, but real all the same) between artistic phenomena belonging to two such diverse and distant worlds, which are historically related despite the fact that they lie at opposite ends of Eurasia. Thus, it is not absurd, after an archaic period that creates long-lasting building and structural prototypes—the Shang and Chou dynasties—to recognize a classical period, in which the emphasis is on spectacular and monumental effects, but also on balance and harmony. So-called classical styles exist in India, flourishing when the local culture rejected suggestions from the Greco-Roman world and reached its own full splendor. After this phase, which corresponds to the four centuries of the Han dynasty, there follows a medieval period that produces elongated forms in sculpture similar to those of our Gothic, and which many, even historically speaking, have considered the exact equivalent of our Middle Ages. This is the period of the Six Dynasties.

The attention paid by the T'ang dynasty to the rediscovery of the classical at the time of the Han phase, together with a typical sense of measure, strength, and harmony, amply justifies equating the new period of imperial splendor with the European Renaissance. Moreover, the spread of Buddhism had already created in wide areas of Asia the conditions for an Asiatic

54. *Shang-ts'un-ling (Honan), remains of wooden chariots in a tomb of the late Chou period.*

55. *Detail of the Great Wall in the Pa-ta-ling area.*

56. *Small ceramic model of a tower,*
Han dynasty (London, British
Museum).

57. *Small ceramic model of a tower,*
Han dynasty (Toronto, Royal Ontario
Museum).

58. Small terra-cotta model of a three-story house, Han dynasty (Kansas City, William Rockhill Nelson Gallery of Art).

59. Sepulchral tile representing a monumental gateway of the Han dynasty. Chengtu (Szechwan), Hsi-ch'eng Museum (from Sickman-Soper, 1956).

humanism that profoundly altered and exalted the value of man. Certain Sung works, especially those of the Northern Sung, still show Renaissance traits, despite the brief interruption caused by the period of the Five Dynasties. Under the Southern Sung and in the barbarian Liao reign, however, we see the appearance of elements of plasticity in decorated surfaces and a concern for chiaroscuro, a variety of architectural features that would pass from a kind of Mannerism to the strong volumetric and chromatic contrasts of the Yüan—and to a certain extent also the Ming—"Baroque." This pseudo-Baroque, simplified in line and enriched by minute and even colored ornamentation, delicately painted flowers, birds, and plants, will change in color from the Ming to the Ching periods to produce a "Little Baroque," a light and fanciful Rococo; in some Ching buildings, particularly the royal palaces, it is even possible to note, as Soper[1] has already done, a kind of delicately structured Neoclassicism.

We can, therefore, assign the essential phases of artistic evolution in general, and of architecture in particular, to various dynasties, which for diverse reasons promoted different architectural trends. It is important to consider these daring but by no means arbitrary correspondences with traditional Western categories before returning to the customary classification by dynasty. The divergence in chronology between China and the West for such classifiable phenomena with the same name is sometimes considerable, but this hypothesis has been drawn primarily as an answer to all those critics who have too hastily judged Chinese architecture as monostylistic. They unwittingly approach absurdity in suggesting a fixed view of an architecture that has undergone three thousand years of development.

Prehistory and Protohistory

Chinese literary sources, thought to be of the late Chou period, refer to a very ancient time when men lived in "holes and nests," presumably caves or dwellings dug in the earth similar to those still used by certain populations living at a primitive level in such northernmost areas of Asia as Korea. In an infinitely more remote period (possibly five hundred thousand years before Christ) the earliest hominid so far discovered on Chinese soil—the *Pithecanthropus* of Choukoutien (*Sinanthropus pekinensis*)—undoubtedly sought shelter in the natural caves and grottoes near Peking, for it is in these caves that remains of skeletons of *Sinanthropus*, already with slight Mongoloid characteristics, have been found. He produced hatchets, knives, and disk-shaped stone scrapers, knew what fire was, and practiced burial rites and probably cannibalism.

In addition to Choukoutien, traces of more recent Paleolithic sites have also been found at Ting-ts'un in Shansi (Ting-ts'un man), at Sjara-osso-gol in the great bend of the Yellow River, in Honan and Szechwan. But it is only in the Neolithic period—that is, from the beginning of the fourth millennium B.C., with the introduction of agriculture and thus of stable settlements—that we have finds of any architectural value. Excavations

60. Stone slab from a Han tomb with
a relief depicting a building (New
York, Metropolitan Museum of Art).

61. Feng-huang (Szechwan),
necropolis, remains of the entrance
portal.

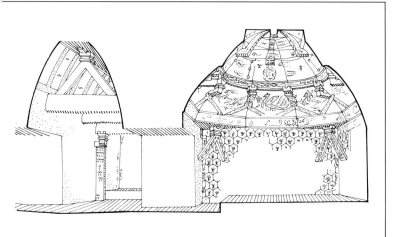

carried out between 1950 and 1955 at Pan-po-ts'un near Sian in Shensi have revealed the existence of an agricultural village, datable to the middle of the third millennium B.C., of already defined characteristics. It has been assigned to the middle phase of the so-called Yangshao, or painted pottery, culture that seems to have developed in the loess lands of the northeast.

The huts are surrounded by a wide ditch, used for drainage and defense, which separates them from the burial grounds. The latter are arranged in a circular or quadrangular fashion, and sunk about a foot and a half into the earth, with a hearth at the center. Four holes around the hearth indicate the presence of wooden columns designed to support the roof, probably consisting of a wooden framework of small beams and completed by straw, branches, or woven reeds, then covered with clay. The conspicuous nature of the roof (which must almost have touched the ground), the custom of having the entrance face south, the wooden pilasters, and above all the presence of the so-called clan house (a spacious rectangular structure situated almost at the center of the village), are significant. They represent the germs of certain characteristics of traditional architecture and urban planning that were to prevail in future centuries, even though the idea of a pounded earth floor dug lower than ground level was discontinued in the historical period.

The villages of the Lungshan, the other great contemporary Chinese Neolithic culture (in some cases superimposed on the Yangshao), show nearly the same configuration. They are, however, often situated on hills and surrounded by a wall of pounded earth, which at Ch'eng-tzu-yai is rectangular in shape and very similar to those of later Shang cities. The tombs, which lie within the wall, consisted of trenches where the body was placed supine along with such funerary trappings as vases, axes, and arrows. This differed from the custom in the northeast, where—for example, at Pai Tao Koi Ping in Kansu—the corpse, again surrounded by funerary offerings, was buried in the fetal position.

Shang Dynasty (1766-1122 B.C.)

Confucianism, with its cult of the antique, contributed to the origin and preservation of a number of historical works dealing with the most archaic phases of Chinese history. According to the oldest sources, Chinese civilization begins with a series of mythical emperors, true cultural heroes, who are said to have invented agriculture, ways to control the flow of rivers, and writing. But no traces of these mythological rulers—or better, of the historical phases to which they correspond—nor of the successive Hsia dynasty, which according to traditional chronology would seem to have lasted from about 2205 to 1766 B.C., have been found by archaeological excavation. The Shang dynasty, which apparently extended its dominions along the middle and lower course of the Yellow River in the regions of Honan, Hopei, Shansi, Shensi, and Shantung, is considered on the basis of archaeological and stratigraphic evidence to follow immediately on the heels of the Neolithic period. Here Chinese history begins. Here the ancient

62. Outskirts of Pyongyang (North Korea), interior of the Tomb of Celestial Kings and Earth Spirits, Koguryo period (from Sickman-Soper, 1956).

63. Li-cheng hsien (Shantung), Shen-t'ung-ssu, square pagoda, period of the Six Dynasties.

64. Mount Sung (Honan), twelve-story pagoda in the Sung-yüeh-ssu complex, period of the Six Dynasties.

legends are confirmed, if only in part, by archaeological finds.

Of the numerous capitals to which, according to tradition, the Shang rulers moved, two at least can be identified—one near Chengchow, which would be the ancient Ao recorded in the *Bamboo Annals* and by Shih'chi, thought today to have been begun around 1500 B.C.; the other at Hsiao-t'un near Anyang. This latter is considered to be the last and most famous capital, the so-called Great Shang, founded according to the *Bamboo Annals* by P'an-Keng in 1300 B.C. It is primarily on this site that the discoveries made by Japanese scholars up until 1937, and later by the Chinese themselves, have made it possible to discern nearly parallel rows of square or rectangular dwellings, presupposing a chessboard pattern of streets, and, more important, spacious terracings of pounded earth for temples, palaces, and other major buildings. These structures had stone foundations (occasionally covered by a surface of bronze) into which wooden pillars must have been inserted, as in the case of the rectangular great hall, some 98 feet in length, in which we find two of the three essential components of Chinese architecture: the terraced foundation, and the supporting structure of wooden columns, securely linked by a series of wooden architraves, and placed—regularly spaced and with a central row—slightly behind the edge of the terrace.

It has even been possible to recognize the outlines of a certain development in Shang architecture. In the older capital near Chengchow, the terracings of buildings were lower and less frequent, while the houses, often with rectangular foundations of from 9 by 5 feet to 52 by 25 feet, had pounded earth floors sunk about a foot and a half below ground level.

Near Anyang, on the other hand, the pounded earth pedestals of the buildings are higher and much more numerous. Though the old type of Neolithic dwelling with its sunken floor survives in many examples, round or square in shape, we nevertheless find buildings that were obviously at ground level; these may mark the moment of transition from the sunken dwelling to that raised on terracing.

The walled city, however, already appears to have taken definite shape: at Ao, near Chengchow, the remains of the wall measure 1 by 1.2 miles in perimeter. At Anyang, the streets form a chessboard pattern and the most important buildings must have been similar in appearance to the future Chou city, even if the roofs most certainly were different, since we find no trace of roof tiles.

The urban structure corresponds to a highly distinct society, a kind of sacred monarchy that extended its rule over the feudatories of other cities and villages, and in which both slavery and human sacrifice were practiced. Indeed, almost all the important buildings exhibit traces in their foundations of human or animal sacrifice. The large royal tombs, along with their rich bronze and ceramic trappings, their chariots and the skeletons of horses, in particular contain numerous remains of decapitated human victims, testifying to a religion that provided for both human sacrifice and the

69. Lüng Men (Honan), complex of cave temples.

70. Changan (Sian, Shensi) remains of the imperial Lin-te-tien pavilion, T'ang dynasty.

survival of the spirit after death. The skeleton of a dog (a chthonic and demonic animal) has been unearthed from the deepest part of the foundations, sure evidence of a special propitiatory or apotropaic rite.

These royal tombs, mainly in the vicinity of Anyang, also show the magical and religious significance that the Shang builders were already attributing to the orientation of their structures. The large tomb of Wu-Kuan Ts'un and the royal necropolis near Hsi-pe Kang reveal the existence of a precise scheme for funerary constructions in which greater importance is given to the southern side where the funeral cortege entered on the occasion of the burial. The sepulcher consisted of a quadrangular chamber, dug deeply into the earth, with two access ramps in the northern and southern sides, sometimes almost 66 feet in length. In the more complex examples, two shorter ramps were added on the eastern and western sides, giving a cruciform shape to the whole. The coffin was placed in the funerary chamber under a wooden structure about 6 1/2 feet high, outside of which lay the bodies of the numerous sacrificial victims. The grave was then filled in with earth and leveled with the surrounding terrain. No traces of any particular elements that would have revealed the presence of the tomb from the outside have been discovered.

Chou Dynasty (1122-255 B.C.)

The advent of the Chou dynasty, which succeeded in expanding its frontiers until it eliminated the former Shang rulers, did not constitute a real cultural or artistic break. On the other hand, it was precisely during this period (the longest ever ascribed to a Chinese dynasty) that political changes occurred that were also to have a marked influence on architecture. Unfortunately, only a very few Chou sites have so far been found, and it is hardly possible to trace a difference between the buildings of the first period of relative internal peace (roughly coinciding with the so-called Western Chou reign, which lasted until 771 B.C.) and those of a later period in which the struggles among various feudal states became increasingly acute—to such a degree that the monarchy was obliged to transfer its capital from the outlying Changan to Loyang (Eastern Chou period, 771-255 B.C.). Thus we are unable to follow the changes in any proper sequence. We can, however, note the results.

Many other changes took place in the period that Chinese texts call that of the "Warring Kingdoms" (480-222 B.C.), when the monarchy was no longer able to control the centrifugal forces of its individual vassal states. This was a time of considerable unrest, but also of great cultural and artistic achievement. The two most influential Chinese philosophers, Confucius, who wrote commentaries on the Chinese classics, and Lao-Tzu, author of the *Tao Te Ching*, are thought to have lived during this period.

Generally speaking, the Western Chou period represents a continuation of the structural and artistic models of the more refined Shang type. The texts mention the transfer of craftsmen from the last Shang capital to the

71. Relief showing a wooden building
in the Ta-yen pagoda at Changan
(Sian, Shansi), T'ang dynasty.

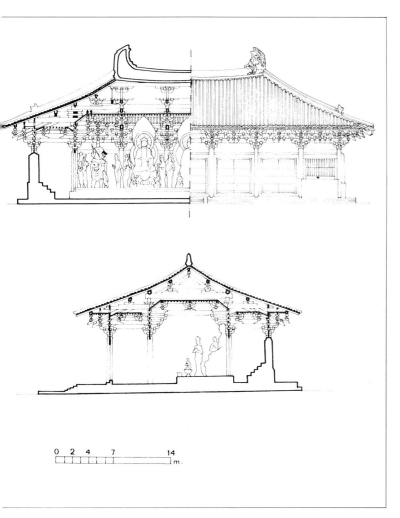

72. *Wu Tai Shan (Shansi), Fo-kuang-ssu, elevation, longitudinal section, and transverse section of principal pavilion, T'ang dynasty (from Sickman-Soper, 1956).*

73. *Fo-kuang-ssu, detail of sloping roof, T'ang dynasty (from Sickman-Soper, 1956).*

74, 75. *Fo-kuang-ssu, details of the interior, T'ang dynasty (from Sickman-Soper, 1956).*

Chou capital, situated near Changan. The plan of the walled city was continued, as well as the custom of burial in underground sepulchral chambers laid out according to rigid geometric and ritual rules. One notes only the greater importance assumed by garrison towns, the military centers of the time, and an attempt to locate urban centers in proximity to the great traffic arteries, a feature that does not hold true for the previous phase. A lesser interest in fortification works is apparent, indicating a temporary feeling of greater security.

As for the tombs, the custom of burial in a sacrificial pit was preserved, as we discover from the tenth-century B.C. tomb excavated near Changan, and those of the necropolis near Loyang (tenth to ninth centuries B.C.).

For the Eastern Chou period and that of the "Warring Kingdoms," the documentation at our disposal is a little more ample; first of all, there are numerous references in the texts to architectural facts and data. As far as theoretical urban planning is concerned, the *Chou Li* [2] contains a highly explicit description of the "ideal capital." It is formed by "a square nine *li* (about 3.6 miles) on each side, with three gates on each side, and nine longitudinal and nine transverse streets, each sufficient in width for the passage of nine chariots. To the left the Ancestral Temple, to the right the Altar of the Earth, to the front the Court, to the rear the Marketplace." The greater complexity of the Chou urban plan as compared to the Shang city is obvious, and there is no doubt that the *Chou Li* anticipates the urban layout of the later imperial capitals. But what is rather indicated by the archaeological evidence from this period is a freer general outline, probably due to the conditions of the terrain and also to the form of pre-existing sites.

Of the capital of Chengchow, near Loyang, there remain only traces of the pounded earth walls, from 10 to 20 feet in width. But the imposing scale of the fortifications found in the capitals of the various kingdoms, especially in the regions of Hopei and Shantung, testifies to a later phase in which there was a serious need for defense. Hsia Tu near I-hsien (Hopei), in the northwestern state of Yen, exhibits a surrounding wall almost 33 feet at the base, with an irregular perimeter, far indeed from the canonical square shape and enclosing a very broad area. This suggests that within the walls in addition to major buildings (of which some fifty foundation platforms have been discovered) and houses, there must also have existed agricultural fields. The plan mentioned in the texts seems to have been more closely executed in the city of the Chao kings, near Han Tan in Hopei; here the quadrangular layout of the colossal walls (about 66 feet at the base and 49 feet in height), and the axial position of the ruins of the major buildings (of which foundation terraces and column bases still remain), contrast nevertheless with the greater proximity of the most important complex to the southern side. This is a marked divergence from the canonical orientation.

Clearly, the *Chou Li* is a theoretical text that does not correspond to the actual situation in the area of urban planning. Similarly, its allusions to the structures and shapes of individual buildings, which turn up also in other

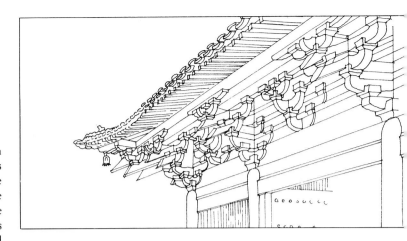

texts, in many cases cannot be taken literally. It is certain that, along with the phenomenon of a gradual development of buildings along a central axis leading to the royal palace, the traditional courtyard arrangement of private dwellings also begins at this time. A ballad in the *Shih Ching* [3] mentions the basic parts of a residence—entrance gate, courtyard, frontal portico of the reception hall—and emphasizes the importance of the courtyard. The texts also point up the magnificence of sculptured and painted decorations, and of brick tilework, the use of which, judging by these sources, would seem to have been widespread from the beginning of the eighth century B.C. The archaeological evidence suggests that such ostentation did not develop prior to the fourth century B.C.; it thus constitutes one of the most significant innovations with respect to the Shang period.

What stands out is the monumental size of carved, painted beams and columns, of the foundation platforms, extensive gardens, and high watchtowers. At the same time, that complex of sumptuary and structural regulations requiring the architectural decoration of each house to correspond to the social rank of its occupants begins to be stabilized.

We can study certain structural characteristics of Chou buildings more closely by examining the incisions on bronze vases. The most important such representation is found on a bowl from a Honan tomb in Hweihsien, though the archaic nature of the rendering raises a number of problems in itself. The two-story building it represents exhibits the typical supporting framework of wooden columns, topped by a tile roof, which does not, however, seem to have the excessive importance in the overall structure of the building that will occur in later constructions. It lacks entirely the characteristic curvature of the slopes of later roofs. The corbel system here seems simplified and reduced to a single block, almost to a wooden capital. On the upper roof, acroteria in the form of goatlike heads may be the prototypes of the very widespread "owl-tailed" acroteria of much later times.

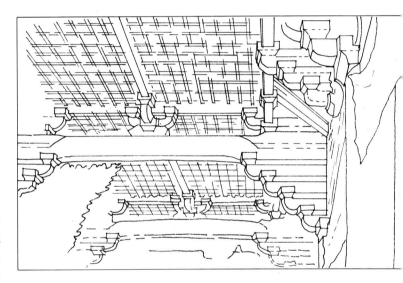

Certain structural details are more difficult to interpret: the foundation platform does not seem to be indicated, perhaps for lack of space, while the upper floor seems to rest on lateral columns rising from a kind of platform, in its turn supported by smaller pillars that rest on the roof of the lower story. It is an anomalous structural solution and hard to explain, unless we ascribe it to a mistaken representation by the engraver, or even to an attempt to show two adjoining buildings in perspective.

Other evidence providing us with direct documentation of the Western Chou period are its tombs, which in general are still close to those of Shang times. However, the practice of sacrificing a dog in the foundations seems to have disappeared, and we can distinguish variations in form and dimension corresponding to the social rank of the deceased, and above all, to local customs. A divergence from the normal scheme is found in the tombs of Tangshan in Hopei, where the wooden coffin is replaced by stone slabs, perhaps foreshadowing the later stone sepulchers of the Han period.

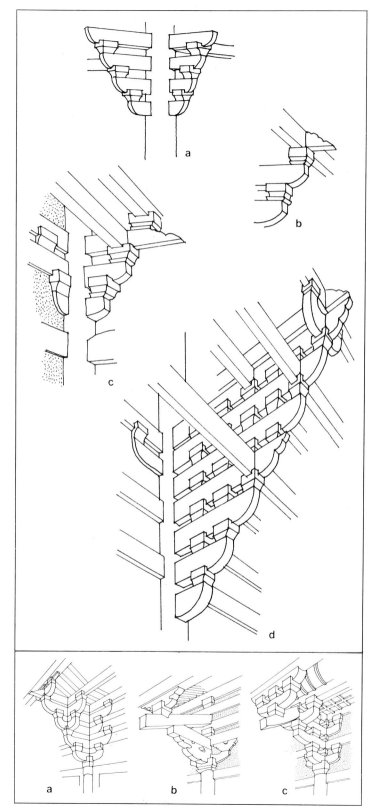

76. Types of bracket systems for wooden buildings: a) Yyng-ch'uan temple in Foochow (Fukien); b) K'ai-yüan temple in Ch'üan-chou (Fukien); c) kaisandō of the Tōdaiji at Nara; d) nandaimon of the Tōdaiji at Nara (from Willetts, 1958).

Other burial grounds have been found in southern regions, where the penetration of northern culture is evident, as at Tung-sun-pa (Szechwan) and at Changsha (Hunan). Here the elaborate design (in wood) of the modestly proportioned funeral chamber (depth, 23 feet; length, 6 to 10 feet; width, 3 to 6 feet) shows the degree of acculturation in this area to currents from the north.

Contrary to the statements of Soper[4] and other scholars, no tombs of the Chou period show traces of the tumuli that were to constitute the characteristic feature of Han burial grounds. Examination of the necropolis situated near Ku-wei-ts'un in Honan—where three tombs of enormous dimensions but similar in shape to the Shang type have been found—has shown that in this period the practice of marking the presence of a sepulcher externally on the surface of the soil had scarcely begun. Tumulus No. 2, in fact, is topped by a layer of pounded earth rising about 20 inches above the level of the terrain, and with a border of large stones placed at intervals; this may constitute a distant prototype (as a surface marker) of the later tumuli.

On the other hand, it is difficult to ascertain the structure of sacred buildings, to which the texts refer often but unclearly and of which the excavations have still not yielded sufficient traces. Probably there were throughout the region altars of pounded earth, square in form and dedicated to the soil in which the victims were buried; or, round and dedicated to the sky under which the victims were burned. But the primitive characteristics of the Ancestral Shrine and of the Ming T'ang (Shining Pavilion), which seems at first to have been the king's residence and later to have become a royal temple, have not been sufficiently reconstructed. Even the Han rulers, anxious to establish the firmest ties with the ancient past, had tried to determine the traditional plan, without, however, being entirely successful. The memory of it had been lost.

It is certain that the shape of the shrine must have been connected with complicated geomantic and ritual rules. And, since the texts mention that the seat (throne) of the emperor was shifted around in the various rooms according to the season, it must surely have been based on astrological requirements as well. But for these ancient shrines, the texts permit us to glimpse only the use of structures and models common to both dwellings and sacred buildings; this is a characteristic feature of all Far Eastern architecture as applied to royal residences intermediate between the temple and the house.

Ch'in Dynasty (255-206 B.C.)

Though this phase covered only a very brief span of time it marked the unification of Chinese territory and the foundation of the Celestian Empire and made a clear break with the past in social, economic, and political areas. There were obvious repercussions for architecture as well. Shih Huang Ti, the First August Emperor (259-210 B.C.), and his minister Li Ssu to an even

77. Examples of the development of the bracket system: a) pavilion of Kuan-yin in the Tu-lo temple at Chi-hsien (Hopei); b) kondō of the Horyuji temple at Nara; c) kondō of the Toshodaiji (from Willetts, 1958).

78. Courtyard in front of the Ta-yen-t'a pagoda, T'ang dynasty.

greater extent, pursued a centralizing and unifying policy that sought to annul completely the centrifugal forces of the old feudal states. While trying to eliminate all ties with the past—hence the persecution of Confucians and the burning of a large portion of the ancient texts in 212 B.C.—they strove to create a truly homogeneous China through the adoption of a single script, a single system of weights and measures, and a great network of roads to facilitate exchanges and contacts as it converged toward the capital, Hsien-Yang in Shensi.

The individual regions were obliged to adopt a single gauge for the wheels of carriages, which so far had differed from state to state and constituted a more serious obstacle than one would think to contacts and exchanges. The deportation of the feudal nobility with their families to the capital (the texts speak of more than one hundred thousand persons) brought interregional characteristics to Hsien-Yang. Thus, the isolation that made the architecture of one state different from that of another came to an end. As Soper rightly states: "It was for the first time possible to compute a sum of Chinese architectural achievements. The next step must have been the fusion of regional differences into what was intended to be a single imperial style."[5] Unfortunately, archaeological excavations have not yielded many traces of this "architectural revolution." Hsien-Yang was in fact burned by the rebels led by Liu Pang, founder of the Han dynasty, and the texts record that the fires lasted for three months. Nevertheless, by examining the artistic production of the successive Han dynasty, we will be able to complete the picture. But the taste for the monumental and the imperial splendor that the texts ascribe to the constructions of Shih Huang Ti is likewise clear from the excessive dimensions of certain buildings. The palace of A-fang, for example, is described by the sources as an immense complex placed among gardens, ponds, and rivers, with its great central hall "five hundred paces from east to west and five hundred feet from north to south."[6] This same taste can be discerned in the emperor's great tomb near Hsien-Yang.

Here the tumulus appears for the first time. It is of colossal dimensions: its square base measured about 980 feet on each side, and the height, according to tradition, was 492 feet.

Another innovation is shown by the presence around the tomb of stone animals about 12 feet high; they seem to have connected the funerary garden (which, according to the texts, extended for more than five *li* around the tomb in the layout of the Han imperial tombs) with an avenue of access or *shên tao* (Road of the Spirits), which was flanked by large stone sculptures. It should be mentioned here that the Chinese *li* is equivalent to about one third of a mile. It has been thought that Shih Huang Ti mobilized all the working resources of the nation for such colossal architectural works in order to avert the danger of new civil wars and secessions.

The texts mention the thousands of workers employed on the Great Wall, another of Shih Huang Ti's grand achievements and one that has come down to us, albeit through later reconstructions (especially the almost total one

carried out in the Ming period). Erected along the northern confines as a bulwark against the nomadic tribes that conducted continual raids on Chinese soil, the Great Wall probably connected old lines of fortifications in pounded earth built for the same reason by the small Chou states. It consists at present of massive stone blocks that form a crenellated wall from 18 to 30 feet high, with watch - and garrison towers at frequent intervals. Though not architecture in the strict sense, the Great Wall, winding slowly along the undulating hills, imparts grace and majesty to the landscape, with which it merges. It thus becomes one of the best examples of the typically Chinese desire to achieve a harmony between the human (in this case, architectural) product and its natural setting.

Han Dynasty (206 or 202 B.C.-A.D. 220)

A dynasty divided into two periods, interrupted by the reign of a usurper, Wang Mang, was to emerge in opposition to revolutionary Ch'in innovations. Though bent on restoring Confucianism and traditional values, the Han dynasty—historically divided into Earlier, or Western, Han (206 or 202 B.C.-A.D. 9) and Later, or Eastern, Han (A.D. 25-220)—did not abandon all the achievements of the First August Emperor, particularly in the field of architecture. What is more, one might even say that Ch'in models, along with those of Shang and Chou, which in the Han period were from time to time patiently sought out in the ancient sources (as we have noted for the case of the Ming T'ang), now arrived at complete maturity. The great Han expansion on the Asian continent, despite occasional setbacks, reached from Korea to the Indochinese peninsula as well as into Central Asia; and led to the spread of Chinese architectural concepts in new territories, where the foundations were laid for continuous and fruitful artistic collaboration. It is precisely for this reason that evidence of Han architectural activity can be drawn not only from the remains existing on national soil, but also from the clues offered by works constructed in conquered areas. We find them in the small terra-cotta models of buildings (*ming-ch'i*) included among burial offerings, in stone reliefs, and particularly in the tombs in the Korean colony of Lo-lang. Numerous historical and poetical writings (for example, those characterized as *fu*, one of the genres of Han poetry) are rich in allusions to monumental buildings, and to the geomantic and sumptuary rules that regulated their construction.

Sufficient traces have been found to define the layout of the two principal capitals, whose sites were chosen for political and military reasons. We can conclude that the Earlier Han capital was located near Changan, and that of the Later Han near Loyang, though naturally the wooden buildings themselves have disappeared.

To whatever extent Changan was built by royal decree, the previous site, as well as the unevenness of the terrain, must have determined the shape of the city walls. They are about 12 miles in length, and do not form a perfect square, the northwest and southeast corners being irregular. And, though

81. Mount Fang (Hopei), small pagoda of Yün-chü-ssu, T'ang dynasty.
82. Shen-t'ung-ssu (Shantung), burial pagoda of Liang-tzu, T'ang dynasty.

71

the principal new streets were laid out in a chessboard pattern according to the old Chou canon, the main axis, starting at the center gate of the southern side, was nevertheless abnormal in that it did not lead to any important palace complex. Actually, the two Han royal palaces, the Wei-yang and the Ch'ang-lo, occupied respectively two almost symmetrical areas to the southwest and southeast. The large sanctuaries and administrative buildings were also irregularly located. On the other hand, the layout of the Later Han capital was closer to the canonical quadrangular plan. According to the texts, the great south-to-north Processional Way rigidly followed the Chou canon and was flanked by government buildings.

The monumental, as the Chinese conceived it, was created by a large number of buildings of ample proportions, mutually related among themselves by arcades, loggias, terraces, staircases, and curtain walls, all in accordance with rules of axiality, symmetry, and rhythm that had already been formulated in the Ch'in period. This monumental effect was pursued as well by the Han rulers as a necessary axiom and manifestation of a stable, centralized government. At the same time, a certain sense of verticality was sought, with elevated structures that enlivened or acted to counterbalance the horizontal mass of the large halls. The texts, small terra-cotta models of buildings, and finally sepulchral reliefs all testify to the existence of structures with such isolated towers as represented by, for example, the ceramic tower in the British Museum. Some towers were placed to the sides of entrance gates; see the sepulchral tile with the representation of a monumental gateway, in the Hsi-ch'eng Museum, Cheng-tu, Szechwan, for an example of this practice.

Various types of these constructions are distinguished in the texts. The oldest, already documented in the Chou period, is the *t'ai*, rising on a high base of pounded earth. The *ch'üeh* (the two elements flanking gateways, and which vary in size from simple pillars to huge watchtowers) seen to belong to the Han period, as does the *lou* especially, an isolated wooden tower documented by numerous small models and perhaps the archetype of the Buddhist pagoda.

The Han remains found in Changan have shown that the extravagant dimensions reported by the texts for the great pavilions of the imperial palaces corresponded to reality. The audience hall of the Wei-yang, which according to the texts measured in plan more than 394 by 115 feet, has been identified on the spot with a platform of pounded earth over 300 feet long and about 49 feet high. Such buildings were often larger than those that came later, while porticoes and foreparts amplified the dimensions still more. Thus, the perimeter of the whole complex could even be measured in miles. Great technical innovations facilitated monumental construction. The corbel system, for example, for which it is impossible to establish a beginning date, seems to have been widely adopted for the first time in this period, and was apparently applied both to architecture in wood and to the translation of this into stone. Certainly the system makes it possible to build

roofs with much wider and heavier tiles. Another great triumph of Han architecture is the devising of stone or brick structures with masterfully connected barrel or ogival vaults, rounded or pointed arches found in the imperial necropolises, and to which civilizations of the West may well have contributed.

Even the use of roofing tiles becomes perfectly defined, as is shown by the terra-cotta *ming-ch'i* in the William Rockhill Nelson Gallery of Art in Kansas City. On the other hand, the texts speak of coffered or actual cupola interiors, though they are not very clear on the disposition of the wooden elements. And, it is certain that the more important Han structures, whether palaces, temples, or monumental gateways, were replete with decorations: the sources describe the carvings and the incrustations of gold and jade, the wall paintings, the sculptures, and the plant and animal ornamental motifs that blended with the architecture itself.

We have a demonstration of this in some of the finest tombs (such as the one at Pei Chai Ts'un in Shantung), in which the entrance, the walls, and the pillars show a continuous decoration in very low or actually scratched relief, so dense as to create the sensation of a *horror vacui*, alien to the taste of classical China. In the tomb near Wangtu in Hopei, there remain traces of extensive wall paintings, representing dignitaries and historical personages, similar to those that, according to the texts, adorned Han palaces. Judging by the remains in our possession, this kind of ornamentation, though dense and sumptuous, did not lead to any disunity in the architectural mass; the flat—one might say, calligraphic—character of the design tended to emphasize and follow the structural elements without detracting from their rhythm.

Even in its tombs, the Han period expressed its inexhaustible fantasy, while remaining faithful to traditional Shang and Chou rules for orientation and symmetry, and adapting innovations proposed by the Ch'in. The introduction of the stone funerary chamber topped by a tumulus, which was adopted more widely under the Later Han (though we still see wooden structures applied in the tomb of General Ho Ch'ü-ping in Shensi), allowed for a more articulated modulation of the plan, with entrance spaces, corridors, and supplementary chambers, as in the two large princely Wangtu tombs in Hopei.

On the outside, the *shên tao* and funerary garden were enriched with pillars, portals, human and animal figures, and small sacrificial temples (*tz'u*) made of stone slabs, on which the masterful decorative skill of the Han was unfolded in all its elegance. The small sacrificial temple of Mount Hsiao-t'ang near Feicheng is the earliest example of such an open-air Chinese building that has come down to us, as are the four little temples of the Wu family necropolis near Kiasiang (Shantung), from Later Han times.

Though their structure is of stone, the interiors of these burial grounds have preserved enough elements to allow us to reconstruct Han wooden architecture as well. In fact, due to the predominantly wooden character

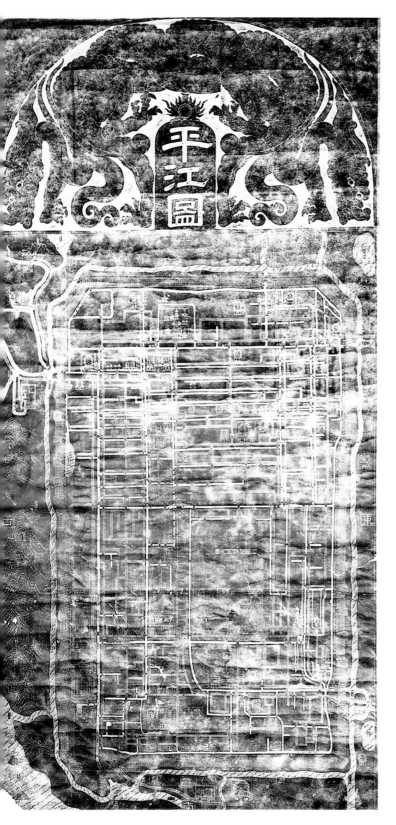

93. *Chin-tz'u, near Yangku (Shansi), Shen-mu tien (Pavilion of the Holy Mother), detail, Sung dynasty.*

94. *a) Plan of the city of Changan, Tang dynasty; b) plan of a complex of Japanese private houses of the Heian period (from Willetts, 1958).*

95. *Yinghsien (Shansi), pagoda of Fo-kuang-ssu, Liao dynasty.*

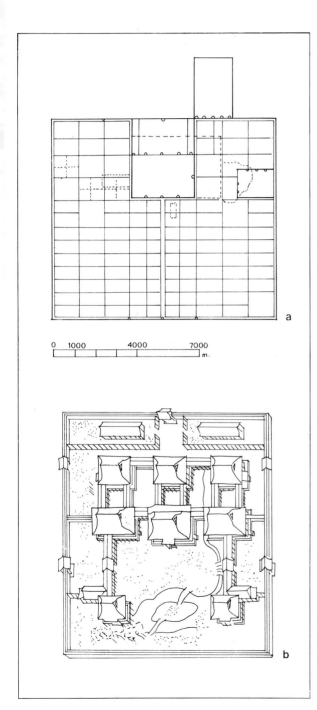

0 1000 4000 7000
m.

96. *Kaifeng (Honan), "Color of Iron Pagoda," Sung dynasty.*

97. *Vertical section of a pavilion (note the excessive bracket system). Diagram of a wooden structure in the so-called Imperial style. From the* Ying-tsao-fa-shih *construction manual, written in the twelfth century by the functionary Li Chieh.*

98. The Return of Lady Wen-chi to China, *by an unknown artist of the Sung dynasty (Boston, Museum of Fine Arts).*

99. Nan-K'ou (Hopei), Chu-yung
gate, Yüan period.

100. Peking, T'ien-ning temple,
octagonal pagoda, Liao dynasty.

of Chinese architecture, these perfect stone constructions very often utilize, with decorative value, typical elements of wooden architecture. Such is the case of the enormous boat-shaped bracket arms, a typically Han feature of the tomb at Pei Cha Ts'un near I-nan in Shantung.

The same tomb, datable to the end of the Han period, has for the first time revealed a type of ceiling that German scholars have called *Laternendecke* (lantern ceiling), and which is constituted of diminishing squares, obliquely placed one within the other.

This ceiling was to find wide application in the later architecture of the Far East. Von Le Coq, and later Soper examining this element of workmanship (in its constructed form but sometimes only as represented pictorially) in western and Central Asia, have advanced the hypothesis that it is derived from wooden roof coverings in Armenia and western Turkestan, whence through numerous intermediate stages to be found in the cave temples of Central Asia it would have reached the Far East. The considerably early date of the I-nan tomb, however, and the fact that the lantern ceiling is here already used as a decorative motif into which rosettes are inserted, suggests an opposite hypothesis. Moreover, the structure, obviously inspired by wooden prototypes, corresponds precisely to the clearest requirements of the Chinese aesthetic—specifically, the superimposition of similar elements—and only serves to confirm our conjecture that this type of ceiling is in reality an invention of the art of Chinese carpentry. There is no reason not to suppose a reverse direction for the diffusion of this type of ceiling, which, from the China of the Han dynasty, would have been carried to the West just as it also arrived in Korea, where it is found, for example, in the great mid-sixth-century Koguryo tomb near Pyongyang.

The architecture of the Han dynasty deserves credit, too, for having conceived the Chinese design for the Buddhist temple, though unfortunately we have only the texts here to rely on. Chapter CIII of the *Hou Han Shu* (the chronicles of the Later Han) tells of a two-storied pavilion surmounted by nine rows of bronze disks, a building that would have been the ancestor of the pagoda. On the other hand, remains of non-Buddhist religious buildings have been found. The Ming T'ang, for example, corresponds exactly to the textual descriptions, which emphasize the central plan, the sequence of circles and squares (symbolic references to heaven and earth), the relevant connections or intersections, the placing of openings at the four cardinal points, the foreparts and interior subdivisions, corresponding to the seasons, months, and days of the year. The foundations, discovered near Changan, of a monumental structure in the form of a Greek cross, superimposed on a square terrace and a broad circular platform, confirm this.

Eight other sanctuaries of this kind (square in shape, however) can be ascribed to the building activities of the usurper Wang Mang, who erected them in honor of his mythical ancestors. They have been uncovered in the capital and demonstrate the widespread acceptance of the centrally planned

sanctuary, which will constitute the archetype of all future "altars" to heaven and earth from the T'ang dynasty to the Ch'ing.

Six Dynasties (A.D. 221-581)

We still know little about the layout of cities during this troubled period, but it can be supposed that in such major sites as Loyang, the Chin capital and later that of the Wei, the Han plan was preserved. A description of the city, primarily of its Buddhist sanctuaries, has come down to us in the *Memories of the Sangharāma of Loyang* by Yang Hsüan-chi. It is substantially the account of a visit made in 547, and confirms this hypothesis.

Nanking, the capital of the southern dynasties, which more than the others kept alive the Han tradition, must also have been close to the traditional plan. Unfortunately, the major part of the monuments at Nanking have sunk into the ground. The necropolis has remained accessible, however. Though not excavated in depth, it shows its derivation from the Han in its tumuli, which are surrounded by an enclosure oriented according to canonical rules.

Since no specimens of wooden architecture remain on Chinese soil, we are obliged to use the sculptured images from tombs or Buddhist cave temples, or else the Korean and Japanese examples that give evidence of the spread of Chinese architecture throughout the Far East, in order to form an idea of the Wooden buildings of this period.

The image of a quadrangular pavilion, very simple in design, with openings at the center of each side—to be found in Cave No. 6 at Yunkang in Shensi (second half of the fifth century)—shows how a third central arm was added to the boat-shaped Han brackets, as well as the evolution of the acroteria that topped the simple double-sloped roof, assuming the classical "owl-tail" form that was later to be adopted on T'ang buildings. The three-armed brackets were then interpolated with wooden supports in the form of an inverted "V." This is a characteristic that we will find in certain seventh- and eighth-century buildings. It appears in the representation of a wooden pavilion on the architrave of the Ta-yen-t'a at Hsi-an-fu, and in the *kondō* as well as on the southern door of the Horyuji at Nara.

In these latter two examples the position of the support (under the balconies) is already of less importance, a sign of the progressive abandonment of the use of this motif, despite the fact that one still sees it represented in the Koguryo tombs at Pyongyang and in the sepulchral stone pagoda of Ching-ts'ang in the Hui-shan-ssu on Mount Sung (Honan), dating from the middle of the eighth century.

The adoption of curved roofs with concave slopes, which seems to have begun at this time, certainly as a contribution of the styles of the south, led to the search for solutions that would allow a greater lateral expansion of the slopes themselves, as can be seen in the Tamamushi shrine in Japan, probably of Korean ancestry.

Such innovations, widely employed by the T'ang, emphasize a body of

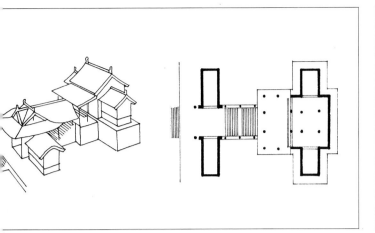

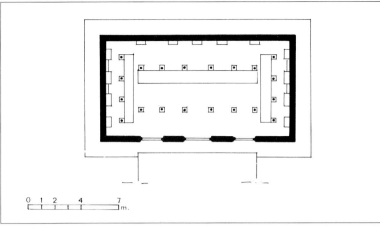

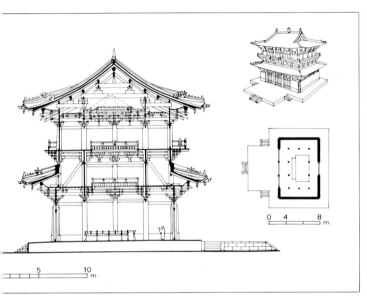

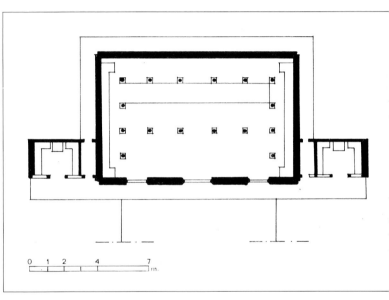

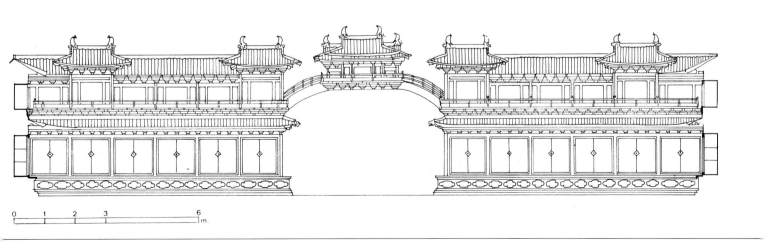

106. *Peking, Miao-ying-ssu, Pai t'a,*
Yüan dynasty.

107. *Peking, pagoda in a bamboo*
garden.
108. *Peking, Pa-li-chuang pagoda,*
detail.

technical knowledge—the science of building, we would call it—and on another level tend to augment an interest in mechanics and automatic devices. The texts mention a "rotating mechanism placed below the ceiling, embellished by a view of the sky, on which celestian bodies were painted,"[7] constructed for the Ming T'ang built by the northern Wei (A.D. 386-534). Other structural innovations were introduced by the so-called Western world. In fact, the "barbarian" states of the north were undoubtedly more open to influences from the West; they were much less subject to Confucian conservatism, and were driven by the new religion of Buddhism to adopt forms of Indian and Central Asian origin that had been created to fulfill the liturgical and doctrinal requirements of Buddhism itself.

In addition to the decorative motifs revealed in the sculptures and paintings from cave temples and tombs, and absolutely unknown to China in previous epochs (such as Classical acanthus leaves, Indian lotus blossoms, capitals with the heads of Persian animals), one might point out the use of entasis in wooden columns, this being perhaps a remote Classical remini-scence. Proof can be seen in the Japanese Horyuji temple complex at Nara, which by now almost all scholars would seem to agree is stylistically derived from the architecture of the Six Dynasties, even though it represents a later reconstruction.

The phenomenon that better than any other demonstrates the ability of the Chinese, or of the barbarians converted to their civilization, to adapt the traditional architectural style to foreign building models is the pagoda. Its genesis is difficult to reconstruct, primarily because the earliest prototypes are unknown. Undoubtedly inspired, both in its sacred function and its structure, by the Indian stupa, it is of two principal types: one in stone or brick, and one in wood. And, if in the stone type the connection with the stupa is more obvious (one must remember that up to this point, with the exception of certain sacrificial chambers, fortifications, and terracings, no open-air stone building had appeared in Chinese architecture), in the wooden type a comparison with the towers of the Han period comes spontaneously to mind. In fact, in the earliest stone examples that have come down to us, the influence of various kinds of shrines elaborated by Indian and Central Asian architecture is evident.

The square pagoda of Shen-t'ung-ssu in Shantung, dating to A.D. 544, is very close to the traditional stupa. It is essentially a cube, with arched openings at the four sides, and a molded entablature to which is added a pyramidal roof topped by the characteristic "owl-tailed" acroteria. Very close to Indian stupas of the Gupta period is the oldest example of a brick pagoda, belonging to the Sung-yüeh-ssu complex on Mount Sung in Honan, datable to the first decades of the sixth century. The characteristic spire shape with its curved line, its twelve-sided base, its second level with columns at the angles and representations of pagodas (similar to the Shen-t'ung-ssu) in the intervening spaces, its series of fifteen diminishing eaves, make it a totally new type of construction for the Far East. Only a single other con-

89

109. *Yen-ngan (Shansi), group of small pagodas of the Ming dynasty.*

110. *Peking, schematic plan of the modern city included within the perimeter of the fifteenth- and sixteenth-century walls encircling it.*

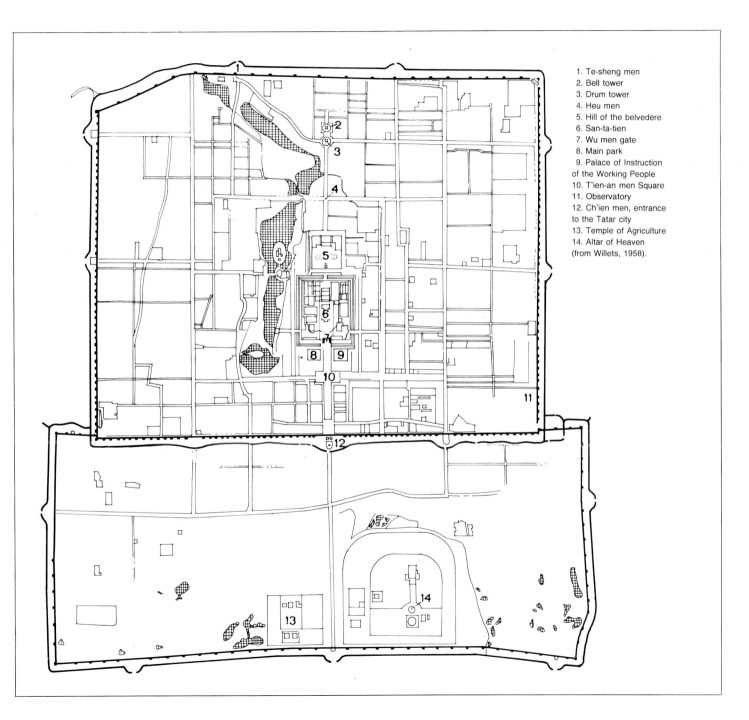

1. Te-sheng men
2. Bell tower
3. Drum tower
4. Heu men
5. Hill of the belvedere
6. San-ta-tien
7. Wu men gate
8. Main park
9. Palace of Instruction of the Working People
10. T'ien-an men Square
11. Observatory
12. Ch'ien men, entrance to the Tatar city
13. Temple of Agriculture
14. Altar of Heaven
(from Willets, 1958).

111. Peking (outskirts), necropolis of the Ming emperors, stela atop a sculptured turtle, part of the tomb of Yung-ling.

temporary example, hexagonal in shape, has been found, in the Wu Tai Shan temple of Fo-kuang-ssu in Shansi, but the later Liao pagodas seem certainly to have been inspired by these early prototypes. More widespread and perhaps even older must have been the single-story type that we frequently find represented in reliefs, on stelae and the walls of caves, such as the one already mentioned in Cave No. 6 at Yunkang. The wooden type of pagoda is closer to Chinese architectural conceptions. The texts agree in describing the numerous installations carried out by the various dynasties, the progressive increase in the number of stories and thus in height, the richness and variety of the decoration and carving. The wooden pagoda, probably inspired by the famous Kanishka tower or stupa erected in the second century A.D. near modern Peshawar, employs this starting point to develop a type of structure directly related to the ancient Chou and Han towers, whose cultural connection with Taoism is likewise underlined by the texts. From the sculptural evidence that we have of these wooden pagodas, we can assume that they were towers square in plan, with roofs supported at every level by columns and corbels. Two striking examples of such representation are the three-storied pagoda shown in relief on the north wall of the Ku-yang cave at Lüng Men (Honan), from the beginning of the sixth century, and the five-storied one sculptured at the center of Cave No. 39 at Yunkang (Shensi), of the late sixth century.

The exceptional vitality of Chinese architecture ensured that even so fundamentally foreign a structure as the stupa would acquire traditional dress, while maintaining the strong tendency toward verticality already apparent in works of northwest India. On the other hand, the other buildings inside the temple enclosure, such as the hall of the Buddhas, the reading hall, and the entrance gates, were to be entirely Chinese in taste. The shape of the temple complex was also to be defined at this time, with the pagoda situated on the axis of the southern entrance gate and followed by the Buddha pavilion and the reading hall, in accordance with the traditional south-to-north orientation. This is shown by the descriptions in such historical texts as the *Wei-shu*. However, another type of layout was to be developed with the pagoda at the center, flanked by the pavilion of the Buddhas and the reading hall, on a line parallel to the side of the entrance. Proof of this has been found in the remains of Korean Buddhist temples from the Koguryo and Pakche reigns, the final result of which was the construction of the Horyuji at Nara in Japan.

Except for stone pagodas, the works that more than any others constituted an architectural novelty were Buddhist cave temples, built according to the plan of analogous Indian and Central Asian ones.

In the oldest caves, especially some of those in the Yunkang group, the Indian *vihara* and *chaitya* are recognizable, with either a central pilaster carved out of the rock in imitation of the central axis of the stupa, or with an actual stupa; while the entrance with its horseshoe arch (*kūdu*) and the use of Classical capitals and Western decorative motifs brings this architec-

ture still closer to its prototypes. In time the typical structures of Chinese wooden constructions would be sculptured or painted on the walls. Corbels, columns, and tile roofs are all reproduced on the rock or painted in the numerous cave temples dug out of mountain cliffs or built in natural caves—at Tunhwang in Kansu, at Lüng Men in Honan—while the entrances sometimes tend to resemble those of Han tumuli. We must not forget that building in caves was by no means alien to the Chinese, as we know from the dwellings dug out of loess in Honan, Shansi, Shensi, and Kansu. There is likewise the evidence of Han rock sepulchers, discovered in Honan and Szechwan, which often display the carved architectural elements of constructed tombs and are preceded by an ordinary vestibule that takes the place of a sacrificial chamber.

Sui (A.D. 589-618) and T'ang (A.D. 618-907) Dynasties

With the reunification of the Chinese nation, it was only natural that, in order to consolidate this unity, the brief Sui dynasty (A.D. 589-618), and to an even greater extent the long-lived T'ang dynasty (A.D. 618-907), should look back to the Han period as the model in all economic, political, cultural, and artistic fields. Nevertheless, the period of the Six Dynasties, though undervalued because of its chaos and instability, had its importance in the development of T'ang architecture. It can even be said that many T'ang structures, particularly Buddhist ones, are a natural derivation from those of the Six Dynasties phase. Moreover, the great territorial expansion of China into Central Asia, Korea, and Indochina, and her relations with the ruling houses of India, Central Asia, and Persia—which also acted as intermediaries with Greco-Roman civilization and later with Islam—brought Chinese architecture, by a process of comparison, to a better knowledge of its own nature and to an improvement of its peculiar characteristics. On the other hand, the introduction and adaptation of new foreign elements, aided by the travels of Buddhist pilgrims, would produce important changes.

As early as the first century of the T'ang dynasty, the characteristics of its particular architectural style take on clear shape. Buildings have ample proportions and a monumental character, and there is an obvious love for clear, linear, and simple forms. In general, these structures, severely functional, are conceived in a spirit of rigorous logic, while in the building plans we witness the realization of the ancient traditional principles, but applied with a new and clear sense of symmetry, rhythm, and harmony. It is not impossible that this search for harmony, rhythm, and clarity was favorably influenced by the development of Chinese music, determined among other things by the success achieved by Central Asian musical groups in the T'ang period, with the greater compositional, rhythmic, and instrumental knowledge that was thereby produced.

Be that as it may, it was to these truly clear urban and architectural forms that the Great Silla Kingdom of Korea and the Japan of the Asuka and Nara

113. Peking (outskirts), necropolis
of the Ming emperors, monumental
entrance portal.
114. Hangchow (Chekiang), Lin Ho
pagoda.

periods were to look, thus achieving in their own territories works that were related among themselves and so obviously inspired by the China of the T'ang that it is not hazardous to speak, for this phase, of an "Eastern pan-Asian" style, with its center in the Chinese capital.

The Japanese city of Nara was built on the plan of the Changan of the T'ang, which was enclosed by a wall 18 by 15 *li*, with the area of the royal palace and government buildings concentrated at the central part of the northern wall, to be approached along the great Processional Way. The rigid axiality of this main artery divided the city into two halves, western and eastern, each with its own central market. The two sections were further subdivided by a chessboard network of streets into rectangular districts, each of which might consist of up to four lesser rectangles separated by narrower streets. Outside the walls to the northeast was another imperial residence— the so-called Ta-ming Palace, which has recently been scientifically excavated and was itself enclosed by ample rectangular walls. This residential complex was symmetrically constructed, as always, adhering to an axis laid out by its major pavilions along a south-to-north line. The monumental entrance to the entire complex was at the south. A less official complex, the Lin-te-tien, situated near the western wall of the Ta-ming-kung and much more varied in shape, is probably the prototype of the freer designs shown by the later "pleasure palaces."

Very few examples of wooden buildings have survived. Remains of the main pavilion of Fo-kuang-ssu on Wu Tai Shan, from the middle of the tenth century, and the Nan-ch'an-ssu in the same area, from 782, still stand, however. In addition, the descriptions provided by historical texts and such chronicles as those of the Japanese pilgrim Ennin, together with sculptured or painted representations (especially those in the Tunhwang caves), and, above all, such remains of the Buddhist complexes of Nara as the Golden Hall of the Tōshōdaiji, allow us to form an adequate picture of the architectural development. The corbel system increases in height, augmenting the number of orders but preserving a solid unity; the use of the *ang* bracket at the corners becomes aesthetically and structurally more coherent; columns slowly lose their entasis. In the Tōshōdaiji *kondō*, they still preserve a slight final swelling, while bases become increasingly elaborate, assuming lotus blossom forms in the middle and late T'ang. On the other hand, toward the roofs, for which the simplified type of slope is preferred, levels are very graduated, with only a slight curvature at the eaves.

An important innovation is shown in the interiors with the progressive adoption of chairs, which had already appeared in China under the Han but were now used more widely, perhaps also due to the influence of foreigners staying in Changan. Up to this time, Chinese interior furnishings had been very similar to the classical Japanese ones that are still in use, but now the elevation of the "working level" ensured the adoption of furniture that would raise the life and activity of the inhabitants from the floor level. Such furnishings, however, unlike in our Western dwellings, were always few

in number, thus leaving the interiors free and uncluttered.

The technical skill of Sui and T'ang builders is further attested by the texts, which record, besides such truly original works as a "rotating pavilion" by Yü-wen K'ai,[8] and a pavilion cooled in the summer by artificial rains, a number of great public works. The Grand Canal, for example, is described as connecting the Yellow River with the Yangtze (A.D. 584 to the end of the eighth century); and the royal palace of Loyang, the other great monumental city of the T'ang, was enhanced by a large artificial lake. An example of this skill and originality survives today in the large reduced arch, flanked by four auxiliary arches, of the Great Stone Bridge (whose span measures about 124 by 24 feet) near Chaohsien in Hopei, the work of the master builder Li Ch'un (sixth to seventh century).

The anti-Buddhist persecutions during the year 845 and during the tenth century, a natural reaction to the ostentation of the large monasteries, destroyed the splendid temples in Changan and Loyang. There still remain, however, as we have seen, a few peripheral temple halls and some brick and stone pagodas, which together with the cave temples of Tunhwang, T'ien-lung Shan, and Lüng Men, as well as the Korean and Japanese complexes, constitute what survives of the great Buddhist architecture of the T'ang period.

The plan of the temple complex increasingly takes the shape of the royal palace, in accordance with a natural development that keeps pace with the acclimatization of foreign elements. The prayer hall, which is seen as a substitute for the imperial audience hall, can now be found, especially in the later shrines, isolated on the axis of the entrance gate. The two pagodas, on the other hand, are placed to the sides of the façade, thus forfeiting their role as fulcrums of the sanctuary. This is the so-called twin-pagoda plan, which is imitated in the temples of the Silla Kingdom and in those at Nara and will be widely followed by the Sung. Lanterns in stone, a new type of two-story pavilion (the *ko*), other pavilions such as the reading hall, symmetrically placed and sometimes even octagonal in shape (the Yumedono in the Horyuji at Nara), completed the complex, which at times assumed the dimensions of a royal palace. The brick pagodas, direct descendants of types from the period of the Six Dynasties, become much more linear and harmonious. They may be cube-shaped, like the small pagoda of Yün-chü-ssu on Mount Fang, of the eighth century; or polygonal, like the Hui-shan-ssu pagodas on Mount Sung, also of the eighth century; or square in plan and with the upper stories slightly diminishing in size, like the splendid seventh-century Ta-yen-t'a of Changan. All of them develop slowly, adopting a type of architectural decoration that increasingly tends to imitate the wooden structures. This trend is evident in the Hsüan-tsang pagoda at Changan and even more so in the octagonal Chung-hsing-ssu pagoda at Chou-hsien (Shantung), which dates to the beginning of the ninth century and is the prototype of later Liao and Sung pagodas.

We have direct testimony for wooden pagodas in the constructions at

X. Peking (outskirts), Temple of the
Five Pagodas (Wu-t'a-ssu), Ming
dynasty.

118. Peking, "Pagoda of Glazed
Ceramic," Ming dynasty.

Nara, such as the Daigoji tower, built in the tenth century, and the older Yakushiji, which are extraordinarily similar to those represented at Tunhwang, square in shape and generally with five diminishing stories. In this period, cosmopolitan and open to contacts from abroad while at the same time attentive to traditional values, a particularly ingenious syncretism can often be observed in every field. We are told of a Ming T'ang built for the empress Wu (A.D. 684-704), with an enormous wooden pillar at the center, clearly derived from the axis of the pagoda. In the great imperial necropolises the traditional shape, with the funerary chamber constructed in brick, shows a strong tendency toward centralization around the main room (square, round, or polygonal); and above all a great wealth of sculptural decoration, which, if it sometimes imitates to perfection a wooden pavilion and windows, often displays the potent and realistic plasticity of the T'ang, as in the sculptured horses in the sacrificial chamber of the tomb of T'ai-hsung (A.D. 627-649) on Mount Chiu-tsun.

Five Dynasties and Liao Dynasty (A.D. 907-1125)

The brief so-called period of the Five Dynasties is highly important for the development of Chinese architecture: it marked a new cultural displacement from the north (invaded by the Khitan and Shat'o barbarians) toward the south, where the northern emigrants were to bring a fresh contribution of the already widespread T'ang culture. Here ambitious canal works were to improve agriculture and increase prosperity, and Arab, Indian, and Persian merchants would carry out a thriving sea commerce. The architecture that developed, while traditional, was at the same time rich in local influences, and would reach its full flowering in the period of the Southern Sung. In the northern regions wars and the succession of barbarian kingdoms that were only superficially assimilated to Chinese culture led to the almost total destruction of Changan and Loyang, while, in the beginning, the only new constructions were banal imitations of the T'ang style. The foreign dynasty that more than any other showed itself capable of originality in architecture and town planning—and this was facilitated by its longevity and a long process of acclimatization—was the Khitan dynasty of the Liao (907-1125). In its native Jehol in Mongolia and in its areas of expansion in Shansi and Hopei, we find many remains of Liao architecture, and in particular traces of the five great capitals. The archaeological evidence, together with the buildings attributed to this period by the sources, make it possible to single out these "barbaric" reinterpretations—sometimes highly successful—of the complicated geomantic and structural rules of the T'ang. Often the façades of the royal palaces are placed east instead of south (probably a reminiscence of the ancient cult of the sun); this innovation is also found in the Buddhist complex of Hua-yen-ssu at Tatung.

The octagonal shape was preferred for the typical Liao brick pagoda, generally seven or thirteen stories in height, permitting a greater modulation of the surfaces by pillars, corbels, niches, and often by reliefs. These reliefs, of animals and divinities, in a tireless search for variety, succeed in transforming at least a few of the numerous pagodas that have come down to us into sculptural treasures, such as the eastern pagoda of Pehchen at Chinhsien (Manchuria), from the middle of the eleventh century. Pagodas closer to the southern borders of the kingdom seem to be less baroque, and thus more susceptible to the linear clarity of the Northern Sung, like that of Yün-chü-ssu on Mount Fang near Peking, which dates back to 1117. Its external walls display only harmonious doors and windows. The first wooden buildings appear to be more traditional. The Kuan-yin-ko of Tu-lo-ssu at Chihsien, in Hopei, from the end of the tenth century, seems to be an imitation of a T'ang prototype, while the five-story wooden pagoda of Fo-kuang-ssu at Yinghsien, in Shansi, from 1058, has strongly projecting roof slopes, demonstrating a development parallel to the one that occurred with the Sung in the transition from the large isolated brackets of the T'ang to a system of smaller and densely repeated ones, in which the use of the *ang* bracket is frequent.

The relationship of dependence that surely existed between at least some wooden structures of the Liao dynasty and those of the contemporary Sung is clearly shown—in a rather unique way—by the *sūtra* cupboards in the library of the lower Hua-yen-ssu at Tatung, which imitate buildings. Here the ideal delicacy of the bracket system—much varied and with multiple elements, together with the harmonious union of different building types, the graceful curvature of the roofs, with chamfers and gable—would suggest that these cabinets were constructed by Liao craftsmen intent on reproducing in this particular type of wooden architecture the peculiar characteristic of the Sung. One might also say that Liao builders found masonry a more congenial means of construction, precisely because it was less linked to an age-old tradition that almost had the power to paralyze them, just as it was to restrict their successors, the Jurchen dynasty of the Chin, to a mere repetitive admiration of the ancient styles.

Nevertheless, in their tombs, the Liao gave proof of extraordinary ability and strong originality by covering the funerary chambers with perfectly constructed cupolas, perhaps in imitation of their old nomadic tents.

Sung Dynasty (A.D. 960-1280)

In its efforts at unification, the Northern Sung dynasty (A.D. 960-1127) looked back to the vanished T'ang dynasty as its ideal. The imposing monumental constructions of the T'ang inspired it to develop, from the middle of the eleventh century on, a happy combination of visual unity and structural agility, and the results were buildings with slender and harmonious lines, elegant and functional at the same time. Only in a later period, especially during the reign of the Southern Sung (1127-1280), did the architectural style tend toward greater elaboration. Columns then became excessively thin, and the increasingly smaller brackets were superimposed one over another to impart to the buildings pronounced contrasts of volume

and chiaroscuro, accentuated by the coloristic effects produced by the use of brightly glazed tiles and by the shadows generated by the bold curves of the roof corners. These are typical characteristics of the architecture of the southern regions, to which the Chinese had been driven back by the advance of the Jurchen. One should not forget, however, that Yü Hao, the famous architect who helped to plan the first Northern Sung capital of Pien-ching, the present Kaifeng, was a southerner. This means that from the beginning of their architectural development, the Sung welcomed and manifested a considerable contribution from the south.

We can get an accurate idea of the suburbs of the Kaifeng of the Sung through the famous scroll painting in the Palace Museum in Peking, the work of Chang Tse-tuan (1085-1145), and can reconstruct the magnificence of its monumental buildings from the enthusiastic descriptions of the Japanese pilgrim Jojin.[9] Multistoried buildings, pagodas, gateways, and ornamental towers attest the Sung preference for vertical structures, while the need to enlarge the city inherited from the T'ang produced irregular alterations in the city walls and street network, though an effort was made to follow the canonical rules as much as possible. Even more irregular was the layout of Hangchow, capital of the Southern Sung and the Kinsai of Marco Polo, who visited it in 1280 and left a description so minute that the plan of the period can be reconstructed.[10] Laced by canals and crisscrossed by bridges that permitted the effective coexistence of a network of streets and one of waterways (a Grand Canal ran parellel to the main artery), Hangchow's royal palace area was placed in an irregular position (to the south), as a concession to the particular conditions of the terrain. The natural variety of the landscape with its lakes and islands, and the way in which the architectural structures were related to the setting, made this Chinese Venice even more fascinating.

Irregularity of plan, in contrast with traditional rules, is also found during this period in temple complexes. The Lung-hsing-ssu, at Cheng-ting-hsien in Hopei, is long and narrow in shape: two pavilions facing each other on the axis are followed by the Mo-mi-tien or Pearl Hall, by another main pavilion (with two bell towers to east and west), and by the drum tower. This is a new disposition, and one that we will find later in the Ming and Ch'ing periods. As for wooden structures, the *Ying-tsao-fa-shih*—the technical construction manual written in 1100 by the functionary Li Chieh (which we have in its entirety; that compiled a century earlier by Yü Hao has been lost)—allows us to reconstruct their development, and to integrate the evidence supplied by surviving Chinese, Korean, and Japanese buildings. The bracket system, highly diversified but rigorously coherent in its structural values, with the brackets well spaced and the *ang* arms more oblique and elegantly exposed, enlivened the whole; the architrave, in section, assumed the shape of a "T," as in the doublestoried twin pavilions of Lung-hsing-ssu at Cheng-ting-hsien (Hopei), of the eleventh century. In some cases, the striving for ornamentation is accentuated, especially in such

small wooden examples as the *sūtra* cupboard in the same temple. These touches break up the functionalism of the bracket structure—which is reduced to the simple exercise of craftsmanship—and create a new type of bracket, crushed and flat, designed to compensate for the exaggerated slenderness of the columns. Later, we will find widespread use of this bracket in Ming and Ching architecture.

As for the Southern Sung, on the other hand, only a few wooden examples survive. But the buildings respectively called *Karayō* (Chinese style) and *Tenjikuyō* (Indian style) in Japan, and *Tap'o* and *Chusimp'o* in Korea, testify to the presence of two currents formed in this period. The first is defined as "imperial," and carries to the extreme the accretion of brackets by useless additions lacking in static value, and imparting graceful curves to the roof slopes, under which the brackets are thickly clustered. We can observe these innovations in embryo in the San-ch'ing-tien of the twelfth-century Taoist sanctuary of Yüan-miao-kuan at Suchow, and more clearly in the Founder's Hall (or *Kaisandō*) of Eihoji near Nagoya in Japan (1352), extraordinary in its composition.

There remain no examples in China of the second, or "Indian," style, called *Tenjikuyō* in Japanese. It perhaps arose in the southerly regions as a reaction to the excessive delicacy of the official style, and may relate to former T'ang prototypes. But the twin pagodas of Ch'üan-chou (Fukien), from the first half of the thirteenth century, repeat in granite the simple, powerful transverse bracket arms embedded above a tall trunk column that is typical of this style, and which we will find in the Keuk-nak Chon of the Pong-chong-sa, at An-dong-kun in Koreas (twelfth to thirteenth centuries), and even more emphatically in the great southern gate of the Tōdaiji at Nara, of the late twelfth century. Given the Sung preference for slender, multistoried structures, it is natural that pagodas in brick should have flourished up to the twelfth century; beginning in the thirteenth century, however, the predominance of the Ch'an sect would limit their construction. Sung pagodas were covered with sculptures and enamel tiles, with imitations of wooden sculpture, and, in the later types, with actual wooden beams and brackets. Nevertheless, the Sung were able to preserve in their pagodas—the "Color of Iron Pagoda" of Kaifeng, from the middle of the eleventh century, is one such striking example—an elegance of line with a compactness and solidity that was not undermined by this excessive ornamentation.

Yüan Dynasty (A.D. 1280-1368)

The "barbarian" spirit that appeared in the Liao period—with its love for ornamentation and for contrasts in volume and chiaroscuro—achieved under the great Mongol dynasty of the Yüan (heirs to the pan-Asianism of Genghis Khan) one of its most complete manifestations. For this very reason, we may consider Yüan architecture a Baroque phase of Chinese architecture. Of course, the term Baroque here signifies a taste for lively surfaces and

120. Ch'u-chou (Ahnwei), "bath" of
Emperor Hung-wu, Ming dynasty.

121. Peking, Altar of Heaven, p'ai-
lous of the entrance road.
122. Peking, Altar of Heaven,
general view, Ming period.

123. Peking, Altar of Heaven,
Pavilion of Annual Prayers (Chi-nien
tien).

124. Peking (outskirts), necropolis of
the Ming emperors, funerary complex
of Yung Lo, stairway.

125. Peking, Forbidden City, T'ai-
miao, Ming dynasty.

for effects of light and shadow, a taste so deeply rooted in the human spirit that it reappears whenever the natural environment allows. It is fortunate that Marco Polo has left us in his *Travels* precise descriptions of the monumentality and richness of Mongol Peking, for few vestiges of its greatness remain.

It is certain that the nomadic Mongol warriors, once they had occupied the city of Peking, imitated the Liao and Sung architectural masterpieces, carrying to maturity an almost fatal evolution toward Baroque forms, but also welcoming numerous foreign elements related to their traditional taste. The regularly shaped pavilion gave way to the composite form, with porticoes, annexes, and galleries to connect the individual parts. The composite aspect of Yüan buildings is accentuated by the different types of roofs used simultaneously, apparent in the Sheng-ku-miao at An-p'ing-hsien in Hopei, from 1309, and in Li Jung-chin's painting of a Yüan "pleasure palace." We also have evidence of circular or irregular pavilions, perhaps the work of Arab master builders who had arrived at the court of the Mongol emperors.

The Tibetan architectural style, so remote in its heaviness from the Chinese, also appears as a result of the protection accorded by the Yüan to Lamaistic Buddhism. Among the most typical examples of this style, we find the Miao-ying-ssu pagoda in Peking (1271), bottle-shaped, and showing a massive round drum devoid of decoration, on which rests a conical roof. Traditional pagodas, on the other hand, are often excessively animated in contour and varied in shape by symmetrical foreparts on the lower stories, like the Kyong-ch'on-sa pagoda at Seoul in Korea, clearly inspired by the Yüan. In this pagoda the movement of the numerous and diversified roof slopes at every level, and the chiaroscuro of the projecting and receding masses well justify the name "Baroque" commonly used to describe it.

Ming Dynasty (A.D. 1368-1644)

Many modern Western scholars, from Fontein[11] to Soper, have seen in Ming and Ch'ing architecture "a prolonged decadence of the art and science of fine building."[12] Paradoxically, the judgment of Western scholars on the late works of Chinese architecture seems to coincide, with certain exceptions, with that expressed by nineteenth-century European "classicists" with regard to our own Baroque and Rococo. Actually, such evaluations cannot be accepted. Ming constructions, far as they are from the strength of the T'ang and the delicate elegance of the Sung that they would seem to claim as their inspiration, nevertheless have a value of their own. Basically linear, Ming buildings reject excessively curved roofs and regular plans. Rigidly symmetrical in layout, they also achieve a highly pleasing blend of several strong elements—simplicity of shape, the monumentality of structural complexes inherited from the T'ang style (to which the Ming looked back with particular interest), and the richness and chiaroscuro typical of the architectural decoration practiced by the Sung, the Liao, and even the Yüan.

The capital, Peking, was formed by the merging of the Yüan or Tartar city with a vast suburb to the south, the Chinese city. In 1564 it was encircled by a wall and then was subsequently divided by the traditional Processional Way, which, running from south to north, arrived at the imperial palaces—the "Forbidden City." Its major buildings were aligned on this central axis, which crossed through various masonry walls under monumental gates that opened onto vast expanses with terraces and stairways, striking the visitor with an almost scenographic impression of grandiose majesty. The imperial necropolises evoked a similar sense of august power. Here, through magnificent wooden and stone portals, the Road of the Spirits, flanked by large marble figures, led to a succession of courtyards and pavilions that imitated the form of the royal palace. This layout consisted of sacrificial halls, of "soul towers"—that is, monumental towers with eschatological meanings—and finally the sepulchral tumulus, the pivot of the complex, where the funerary chamber with its numerous annexes was located. In Peking, the refined construction technique of the period is clearly shown in its large craftsmanship productions as well as in the Ming preference for masonry structures.

Ming military architecture is demonstrated by its large walls and fortifications; it is to the Ming that we owe the reconstruction of the Great Wall and of many city walls that still survive today. The typical monumental gateways of the period and even the watchtowers often consist of a wooden pavilion of several stories built on a massive platform base of brick masonry, pierced by a wide barrel-vaulted gate and with staircases and balustrades. The so-called Bell Tower of Hsi-an-fu, one such structure, achieves a surprising harmony in the contrast between its closed and imposing lower part and the light and airy upper structure.

Within the framework of this interest (both technical and aesthetic) in brick constructions, we may include such imitations of the Tibetan stupa, the *chorten*—which had first appeared under the Yüan—as the Sarire-stupa of Ching-ming-ssu near Yangku (formerly Taiyüan), dating from 1385, and the arbitrary replica of the very famous Indian temple of Mahabodhi at Buddh Gaya, carried out in the Wu-t'a-ssu near Peking, a massive parallelepiped in masonry surmounted by five pyramidal pagodas, one at the center and the other four at the corners—an obvious reference to cosmological theories.

Traditional pagodas, however, were often miniature in size, becoming small monuments no higher than the sculptured lanterns placed in the courtyards of Buddhist temples. Perhaps an indirect Western influence of European missionaries is discernible in the appearance of two temples constructed of brick and covered by barrel vaults in the Shung-t'a-ssu at Yangku and at Suchow. Both date from the end of the sixteenth century.

As we know, it was at this time that buildings of a European type were erected in China—the Catholic churches built by Father Matteo Ricci and the colonial establishments of Macao and Canton. But aside from the two

127. Peking, Wu men, monumental
entrance gate to the Forbidden City.

128. Peking, Forbidden City, detail
of a building.

129. Peking, Wu men gate as seen
from the north (from inside the
Forbidden City).

130. *Peking, Forbidden City, T'ai-ho
tien, detail of a marble balustrade,
Ch'ing dynasty.*

XI. Peking, Altar of Heaven, p'ai-
lous *of the entrance road.*

132. *Yangku (Shansi), twin pagodas of Ying-tsu-ssu, Ming dynasty.*

133. *Peking, Forbidden City, T'ai-ho tien.*

136. Peking, Forbidden City, Pao-ho tien, access stairway, Ch'ing dynasty.

brick temple structures described—which may also have been the result of contacts with the Indian or Arab world—no important traces of Western influence have been found in the architecture of the period.

Still, much earlier, in the middle of the Yüan period, Giovanni di Montecorvino had at least two Catholic cathedrals constructed in a Gothic style, using, however, Chinese materials and wall coverings of glazed tiles.

Apart from the two archaeological remains, and the steady recognition on the part of the Chinese of their technical interest in the lessons of Western builders, there is no sign of any vaster or deeper influences. Chinese architecture is separated from the West by taste, a different sense of space, by completely different sociological implications—and even by a divergent appreciation of the visual effect produced by architectural structures, which must, of course, be appropriately placed in their natural surroundings. For these reasons, foreign influences that were not sustained by religion evoked little interest among the Chinese and were very limited in scope. They were, basically, lessons in technique that produced no echoes in the taste or standards of a compact civilization so substantially proud of itself as that of the Chinese.

Returning to the traditional line of development, wooden architecture showed a new symmetrical and rhythmic equilibrium, owing to spatial modifications (width of the intercolumniation in the central part of the construction). Lesser importance was given to the factor of traditional bracketing in the structural economy of the building as regards the lower architrave (which was richly decorated) and the two flat brackets embedded at the sides of the columns, which we have already seen appear under the Sung. The bracketing, however, preserves the "grape cluster" form, achieved by the superimposition of secondary brackets—multiplying the number of supporting arms—on the lower central one, on which the main support was concentrated.

These innovations are to be seen in the three ceremonial halls of the Forbidden City in Peking. Aligned on a south-to-north axis, along a gigantic courtyard of about 200 square yards, these halls rise on high and majestic terracings with several enclosed levels, with delicate balustrades of white marble and enlivened by many staircases, which also serve as a symbolic reference to the inaccessible charisma of the imperial power. Reconstructed in 1700, the three halls recapture perfectly the style of Ming buildings of a century before (1627).

Ch'ing Dynasty (A.D. 1644-1912)

However much the Manchu dynasty of the Ch'ing had affirmed since the first years of its rule its clear and absolute wish not to allow itself to be assimilated to Chinese culture, but indeed to impose its own customs on the Chinese, it was inevitable that in the field of architecture no real break occurred. Since the Manchus had no real tradition of their own, there took place simply a development of the Ming style toward less monumental

forms, which were also to be more vividly colored and copiously decorated with paintings (of flowers and birds), with carving and sculpture both in wood and stone, and with enamel tiles.

As had happened in past periods of domination by foreign "barbarians," the Manchus proved to be open to new architectural forms originating in the most diverse countries. The Tibetan style of architecture, though not new in China, had never been so widespread as at the time, and was related primarily to the trend of Lamaistic Buddhism. It is amply demonstrated by the building complexes of Jehol, the northern capital, and the bottle-shaped pagodas scattered through the gardens of Peking—which were often covered with enamel tiles, like the Pai-t'a of the Pei-Hai, dating from 1651, and including characteristic masonry structures with small trapezoidal windows on the Wan-shou-shan near Peking. Owing to the lack of a true Manchu tradition, Western influences were more easily absorbed. This is especially apparent in the Yüan-ming-yüan, the complex of pavilions and park built by Ch'ien Lung, Ch'ing emperor from 1736 to 1796. It is a singular transplantation, the work of two Europeans (the Jesuits Giuseppe Castiglione and Jean-Denis Attiret), commissioned by the emperor to "build in the European fashion." Elements of Western Rococo are grafted onto such traditional Chinese architectural forms as terracings and curved roofs.

This unusual experiment, corresponding in the reverse sense to the Western taste for chinoiserie, gave rise to works endowed with a certain exotic charm, whether from the standpoint of a Western critic observing the effect of the Chinese component, or that of a Chinese evaluating the effect of the Western.

The great imperial "pleasure palaces" were, however, the preferred field for architectural experiments by the Manchus, and in specific cases a particular exoticism was sought. But even elsewhere—in the vast gardens thronged by structures of the most varied forms, with round, polygonal, and multilinear pavilions, with galleries and bridges, and with the insistent use of round, polygonal, lobate, or ogival apertures in the various walls—the will to experiment is obvious. Sometimes Manchu creations can be defined as true caprices—for example, the marble boat with tall shafts raised on a masonry hull and moored in a pool of water in the new nineteenth-century Summer Palace.

The numerous pagodas scattered throughout the royal parks (more as elegant decorations that as places of worship) are often covered with enamel tiles. They resume the niche motif and the polygonal shape used by the Sung, but now the sides of the polygonal are of unequal measure, the wider faces alternating with narrower ones, creating a broken rhythm (which we also find in wooden colonnades). This is to be seen especially in the Pao-liu-li-t'a pagoda of the Summer Palace in Peking—a true jewel, finely chiseled and surmounted by a finial that, while not conflicting with the whole, is similar to the finials of the Tibetan *chorten*. Here it exists in a Chinese copy that is another interesting demonstration of the exotic taste and wish for variety

147. *Peking, Temple of the Ten Thousand Buddhas, detail.*

148. *Page from the* Kung-ch'eng-tso-fa, *an architectural manual published in 1733 by the Ministry of Public Works, Ch'ing dynasty.*

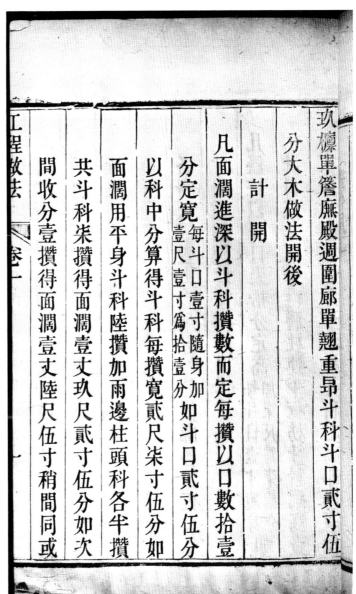

149. Peking, walls of the Tatar city. Ming dynasty.

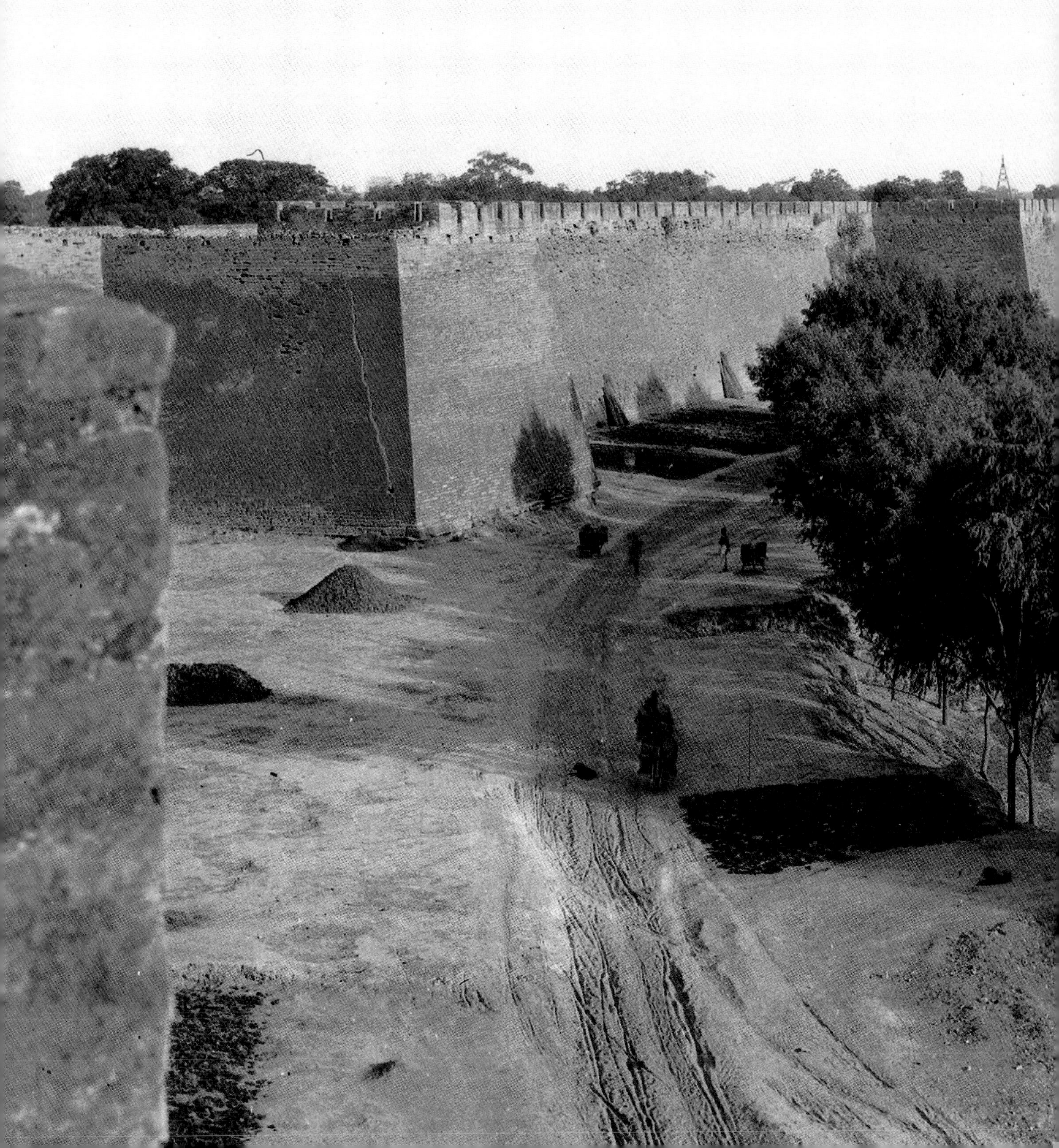

150. *Peking, Pei-Hai, kiosks and gardens, Ch'ing dynasty.*

151. *Peking, Yüan-ming-yüan (Garden of Perpetual Light), Western-style building, Ch'ing dynasty.*

152. *Peking, Pei-Hai, access stairway to the Pai-t'a, Ch'ing dynasty.*

153. *Jehol (Mongolia), Hsu-mi Fu-shou, detail of a roof, Ch'ing dynasty.*

154. *Jehol (Mongolia), Hsu-mi Fu-shou, detail of an acroterion, Ch'ing dynasty.*

155. *Suchow (Kiangsu), Cho-cheng-yuan garden wall with "moon opening."*

156. *Suchow (Kiangsu), Cho-cheng-yuan garden.*

157. *Peking, Temple of the Lamas, bridge between two buildings.*

158. Peking, Summer Palace, bridge
with seventeen arches, Ch'ing dynasty.

159. Peking, Summer Palace,
Fohsiang ko.

XIII. Peking, Forbidden City, T'ai-
ho lien, detail of marble
balaustrade, Ch'ing dynasty.

XIV. Suchow (Kiangsu), Buddhist temple, central pavilion in the Hsi-yuan (western garden).

161. Peking, Summer Palace, interior of the gallery along the lake.

162. Peking, Summer Palace, garden
pavilion, Ch'ing dynasty.

163. Suchow (Kiangsu), Buddhist ▷
temple, central pavilion in the Hsi-
yuan (western garden).

typical of the Ch'ing. Inside the capital of Peking, however, the tendency toward axiality and the symmetrical structures typical of the Ming were preserved. The classic example is that of the complex centered on the Altar of Heaven, culminating in a circular building with obvious cosmological references in its structure, and which, while preserving the characteristics of the original construction (in 1421, under the emperor Young Lo), owes its present appearance to the radical restoration carried out by the emperor Ch'ien Lung in 1754. In the sequence of round and square courtyards, terraces, and staircases reappear the age-gold, rigidly traditional geomantic and ritual rules, which the Ming had made concrete and Ch'ien Lung here rendered with still greater clarity. In wooden buildings, for which we have an exhaustive treatise in the Kung-ch'eng-tso-fa, compiled by a Ch'ing minister of public works, there is a complete loss of the structural value of the bracket system; it is now reduced to a continuous cornice of wooden ribs, at times actually covered by a long carved plank with a "cloud" motif that hides them like a valance. It is exemplified in the eighteenth-century Wan-fu-ko of the Young-ho-kung in Peking.

The exaggerated slenderness of the columns, often reduced to thin pilasters quadrangular in section, required the constant use of the type of bracket with a flattened capital, such as we first noticed under the Sung, elegantly decorated with scrolls and painted.

Such tasteful slenderness in wooden constructions and the consequent small scale of the buildings were a directed result of the extensive deforestation carried out under the Ming. For the Pavilion of Annual Prayers of the Altar of Heaven in Peking, built at the end of the nineteenth century, it was necessary to send to the United States (to the state of Oregon) for timber large enough for the construction of columns of the traditional size. The lack or grave scarcity of suitable lumber was by now an insurmountable obstacle for an architecture that for three millennia had expressed itself primarily in the harmony of its wooden structures.

Modern Period (1912-   )

The Chinese encounter with the modern Western technological world was rendered more violent by the long centuries of proud isolation that had preceded it. At first, beginning in the middle of the nineteenth century, recognition by the Chinese of their own scientific and technical inferiority was so profound that in their new works, inspired by European and American constructions, there was no suggestion of the ancient architecture of China.

This anxiety to adopt wholesale a Western way of life, which is apparent in the first reformers led by K'ang Yu-wei (1858-1927), also had repercussions in the field of architecture. The results were structures in an eclectic style, derived strictly from buildings in the foreign colonial concession, which offered no better examples than the absurd Neo-Gothic Town Hall of the British concession at Tientsin.

Only in 1920, coinciding with the social and political turning point characterized by the spread of nationalism that followed the first struggles of the Kuomintang, did a new style appear that tended toward the reassessment of traditional values. This was the so-called Chinese Revival. However, except for a few valid examples, such as the Chung Shan Hospital in Shanghai (1937), a true merging of Western building methods and techniques with typically Chinese traditional structures was not achieved. Liang-Ssu-ch'eng[13] has rightly observed that there were only to be foreign buildings covered by Chinese roofs.

This movement nevertheless deserves credit for having led Chinese architects toward a historical perspective of their own. In fact, immediately after the chaos of World War II, the search for a national style in architecture seemed to emerge, while naturally not excluding the presence of the major contemporary trend—the so-called International Style—and, to a lesser degree, that of Soviet classicism.

For the moment, it would seem that the more interesting experiments have been conducted in the sphere of the International trend. Buildings have been constructed that recall only by their love for symmetry and by the repetition induced by single structural standards the ancient artistic and traditional forms. This is obviously a poor result. In other cases, Western structures have been blended with suggestions offered—one might say, accidentally—by particular pre-existing masonry buildings already instilled with the Chinese tradition. It is a question of the exploitation of an outlying heritage little known for architectural forms, which draws on Hakka dwellings, on those of the Anhui region, or tries to renew the so-called Tibetan style.

One recalls, however, that the most tenacious characteristics of traditional Chinese architecture are, at least in certain respects, extremely close to the most modern theories of building and city planning. For a long time, there have existed in China a flexibility in the town plan, a tendency toward decentralization, urban expansion by the aggregation of fixed units, the mobility and prefabrication of buildings (given their wooden structure), and the use of a precise standard—the chien, the basic unit of construction derived from the width of the central beam. It is thus perfectly possible that from this point of departure, from these realized objectives, a true and profound "Chinese Revival" may emerge in the future.

Paola Mortari Vergara Caffarelli

137

Unfortunately, only a very few ancient examples survive of the architecture of the Korean peninsula. The material of which many of its buildings were constructed have long since deteriorated, and continual devastating wars, invasions, and destruction have wracked the whole territory of Korea in the course of centuries.

A threefold relationship of borrowing, assimilation, and exchange with the two great neighboring architectural traditions—the Japanese, and above all, the Chinese—characterizes the architecture of Korea. The conception of architecture not as an art but as a craft—that is, an expression not of the desire to create aesthetically valid forms, but rather of a response to practical, functional, and also traditional needs—is common to the whole Far East. This is not to deny that love for structural equilibrium, concern for detail and decoration, and for harmonious placing of the architectural work in its natural surroundings have ensured that from the modern point of view Far Eastern constructions not only have a specific artistic value of their own, but actually anticipate by centuries some of our present architectural and city-planning concepts.

The cities—with their tendency toward a chessboard pattern of streets, flexibility of plan (owing to the deliberate presence of empty areas inside the city walls), decentralization (every quarter with a marketplace and administrative and religious buildings of its own), expansion by the aggregation of small fixed units (the classical family dwelling), and even the mobility of their buildings (given the notable facility by which wooden structures can be assembled and dismantled)—offer infinite points of contact with the most modern urban complexes.

In its more purely structural and aesthetic conceptions, Far Eastern architecture reveals a surprising modernity. For proof of this we need only examine our interest in traditional Japanese architecture and the manifold influence of, and the acclaim received by, modern Japanese masters in Europe and America. The application of a basic standard or measure, derived from the space between supporting columns (which in Korean is called *kan* and corresponds to 10.83 by 10.83 feet), and the use of similar construction elements superimposed or juxtaposed over one another in accordance with precise proportions and relationships, have both been taken up by various modern architects from Frank Lloyd Wright to Helmut Hentrich.

Despite such correspondences with modern architectural thought, it is clear that the architecture of the whole Far East has always had independent characteristics, to be distinguished according to successive periods and different national entities, and sometimes opposed to those of the West.

The architecture of Korea, while closely linked to the Chinese, from which since earliest times and for the entire course of its history it accepted methods and examples of construction, nevertheless developed in an independent manner; these foreign models were transformed according to Korean requirements of taste, tradition, and climate. Thus, the open arcades

164. Puyo, stone pagoda erected by the Chinese general Su Ting-fang, Pakche Kingdom.

165. Kyongju, pagoda of Punhwang-sa, Old Silla Kingdom.

166. Kyongju, Sukka pagoda, Great Silla Kingdom.

with wooden columns that surround the most common Chinese type of building, the *tien* (the rectangular pavilion on a high base, topped by a conspicuous roof), in Korea preserve their primitive structural lines but are almost always closed by a continuous, thin masonry wall, or one of light wooden planks, in order to meet the needs of the more severe climate.

Ancient elements of aboriginal cultures also appear. Often they are utilitarian, like the type of heating called *ondol* ("hot pavement") that utilizes pipes for steam and heat placed under the floor, and which already existed in the protohistorical period. At times these elements are simply traditional, such as the reminiscences of primitive log huts; or, finally, of a religious nature. The habit of orienting dwellings with the entrance to the south, for example, has been observed in prehistoric underground houses.

But it is primarily in the refined way in which buildings are adapted to nature, common to the whole Far East but outstanding in Korea, that the essence of Korean architectural concepts is expressed. It is apparent in the plan of the cities, which, though constructed on the model of the Chinese, do not acquire the fixed rigidity of imperial prototypes; rather they follow the contours of the terrain with greater freedom, both in the line of the city walls and in the layout of the streets. The ornamentation of buildings never attains the overloaded heaviness or exaggerated chromatic vivacity of late Chinese architecture, maintaining instead a smooth and free surface in accordance with a taste for archaic simplicity. The use of natural—that is to say, uncolored—materials for construction (wood, tile, stone) and the restricted chromatic scale they offer contribute to a greater sense of blending with the colors and forms of the natural surroundings.

Prehistory

The scarcity of archaeological evidence on prehistoric structures in Korea—even the ethnic composition of its early inhabitants is in doubt, since it would seem that the Tungusic population was overlaid by migrations from Southeast Asia—makes it necessary to resort to the uncertain data reported in ancient Chinese texts. Above all, we must examine attentively those constructions of an ethnological type that are still in use. All that archaeological excavations have brought to light in the northeast are pit dwellings, circular spaces 13 to 16 feet in diameter with a hearth at the center. In the more western areas preference for the square plan has been noted, as well as the existence of well-defined street connections, suggesting a high degree of village activity. Such finds are in accord with the descriptions in the Chinese annals. They mention, besides the type of dwelling consisting of log huts (still used today in mountain forests), houses dug in the subsoil with a tumulus roof (of which examples remain even in the outskirts of Seoul); and the characteristic habitations of coastal fishermen, constructed always in the form of pits and covered with heaps of conch shells. These, too, are to be found in more northern areas and are related to the prehistoric cultures at the ethnological level of the whole

170. Kyongju, temple of Pulguk-sa, entrance staircase, Great Silla Kingdom.

171. *Wol-ssong Kun, near Kyongju, rock temple of Sokkulam, Great Silla Kingdom.*

172. *Kyongju, Tabo pagoda, Great Silla Kingdom.*

coastal strip and the islands of the Far East. In the religious sphere there are remains of dolmens, attesting probably to the existence of a special form of shamanism together with a cult of the spirits, the so-called Kwisin (demons and gods), which still exists today and takes the form of the *shang-sung*: large tree trunks carved with terrifying faces, very similar to the totem poles of North America; and the *sodo*, posts surmounted by a crudely sculptured bird.

Lo-lang Colony (108 B.C.-A.D. 313)

Though ancient legends state that in 1122 B.C. Ki Tse (Ki Ja in Korean), a member of the royal house of the Shang, established his rule in Korea after fleeing from China with five thousand followers, no trace has been found of this first Chinese settlement. On the other hand, the presence of Chinese colonies during the Han dynasty in the northwest areas of Korea is well documented—in the provinces of Lo-lang (Nang-nang in Korean), Hsiian-tu, Chen-fen, and Lin t'un, which, according to Chinese texts, were founded around 108 B.C.

This first significant entry of Chinese architectural elements occurs precisely in the Han period at a time when the old Shang and Chou building and city-planning standards had arrived at complete maturity.

Actually, an urban complex of the Chinese has been discovered at the

173. Ui-song, five-story pagoda, Great Silla Kingdom.
174. An-dong Kun, seven-story brick pagoda, Great Silla Kingdom.

175. Kyongju, Ch'om-song-dai (Observatory), Great Silla Kingdom.

Lo-lang site near Pyongyang. Its form is a little irregular, with a high platform in pounded earth to support the ceremonial hall, with the foundations of other structures, and in particular a necropolis whose plan, structural elements, and even architectural decoration all indicate a direct contact with the mother country. It thus represents a phase in which foreign models were simply accepted and executed by immigrant specialists, with probably only a few Korean craftsmen involved. Nevertheless, even this phase has its importance in the development of Korean architecture, since it constitutes the matrix from which Chinese architectural concepts were diffused all over the territory of the peninsula. The influence was not restricted to just the neighboring Koguryo Kingdom, which was later to absorb the Chinese colonies; it reached even the tribal states of the south, Ma-han, Sin-han, and Pyon-han, that were to take shape in the historical period of the Pakche and Silla kingdoms.

Three Kingdoms Period (57 B.C.-A.D. 668)

This is the span of time during which Korean civilization, as a result of its encounter with the Chinese, slowly acquired an awareness of its own values. This does not diminish the fact that in the architectural sphere skilled Korean craftsmen of the three kingdoms into which the peninsula was divided—Koguryo in the north, Pakche in the southwest, and Silla in the southeast—were limited in the beginning to a mere effort at assimilation. Actually, the task that the Koreans had to accomplish was a very arduous one. One thinks of the differences in building types and the symbolic implications of Buddhism, of the complicated sumptuary and structural rules required by Confucianism, and, to a lesser extent, the geomantic and magical conceptions of Taoism. The Koguryo Kingdom, which even extended into vast areas of Manchuria, was more prepared for this assimilation, also because of the presence of Chinese colonists on its soil. The wall decorations discovered in the necropolises of the two capitals—one situated in the T'ung-kou district of Manchuria, the other at Pyongyang—represent pavilions, monumental complexes, religious and reception halls; they imitate all the structural and characteristic elements of contemporary Chinese architecture, especially of the northern Wei period (A.D. 386-534). Inside the burial chambers, dug in the soil and topped by a tumulus of earth or squared stones, we find the representation of such false supporting elements of wooden buildings as columns, architraves, and corbels. These are features that, together with "lantern" ceilings—as in the famous and splendidly decorated "Tomb of the Two Columns" in Pyongyang—show a clear derivation from Chinese prototypes. The foundations of an octagonal pagoda and of three other rectangular buildings (religious and reading halls, etc.) surrounding it, discovered in 1937 near Pyongyang, show how Buddhist temples had already reached a typical monumental scale; similar traces have been found in Puyo, the capital of the Pakche Kingdom. But it is in Japan, in the Horyuji complex near Nara, that we still find intact despite successive fires what the

176. Kyongju, "ice house," Li dynasty.
177. Kyongju, tomb of King Wousang.
178. Kyongju, tomb of King Wousang, entrance avenue.

176. Kyongju, "ice house," Li dynasty.
177. Kyongju, tomb of King Wousang.

178. Kyongju, tomb of King Wousang, entrance avenue.

Japanese call the Kudara plan (from the name given in Japan to the kingdom of Pakche). The layout of the Korean temples of this period introduced by Pakche builders into Japan is classic: the pagoda and main hall are situated on the same axis and oriented orthogonally with respect to the entrance. The so-called Tamamushi shrine, also in the Horyuji, seems likewise to have had the same Korean origin; the decoration with iridescent beetle wings is typical of southern Korea. In any case, it repeats, on a reduced scale, the harmonious lines and measured sense of proportion of contemporary buildings.

It was in fact by being filtered through and re-elaborated in Korea that Chinese art, culture, and civilization reached Japan in this early period, just as more Western art and culture, the Indian and Central Asian, had arrived in Korea by way of China.

On the other hand, we have some examples of stone architecture, primarily in granite, from the Pakche and Silla kingdoms. The two seventh-century pagodas in the complexes of Miruk-sa at Iksankun and of Chong-nim-sa at Puyo in the Pakche Kingdom are the oldest examples that have come down to us, and repeat in stone the shape and supporting structures of similar Chinese and Korean wooden buildings. They are square in plan and rise in diminishing levels, with false pillars, architraves, and roofs whose corners are slightly curved. Meanwhile the Punhwang-sa pagoda at Kyongju, capital of the Old Silla Kingdom, takes as its model the brick pagodas of the T'ang dynasty. Built of stones cut in the form of bricks, it shows a majestic simplicity and harmony in its overall purity of line and geometric unity, a prelude to later religious structures.

Great Silla Kingdom (A.D. 668-935)

The Silla government played a unifying role and promoted a great artistic flowering, which also owed much to the adoption of Buddhism as the state religion. This was the classical period of Korean architecture, which, while belonging to the style that Japanese scholars call "pan-East Asian" that initially emerged in the China of the T'ang dynasty, succeeded in acquiring autonomy. It became so through certain definitions of type and structure in its various buildings, through certain peculiarities of shape, and primarily by a harmonious and measured sense of proportion among its different structures. In stone pagodas (*t'ap*), beginning in the second half of the sixth century, a happy and highly original compromise was achieved between the two previous kinds that they were intended, respectively, to imitate: those in wood and those in brick. Thus the so-called Silla type of pagoda emerged, square in plan, generally with three diminishing stories on a pedestal of two levels and topped by a high finial, of which numerous examples remain, such as the twin pagodas of Kam-cun-sa at Wol-ssong Kun. And even though, beginning in the eighth century, the pedestals and stories were to be decorated with figures of divinities, while the whole acquired a greater vertical thrust, this did not alter the linear harmony of the building. The

179. *Yongju Kun, Pu-sok-sa monastery, exterior of the main building, Koryo period.*
180. *Seoul, Kyong-bok palace,* pudo *of the monk Hong-pob, Koryo period.*

XVII. *Yonju Kun, Pu-sok-sa monastery, stone lantern and detail of exterior of the main building, Koryo period.*

181. Yongju Kun, Pu-sok-sa
monastery, interior of the main
building, Koryo period.

As for the sumptuous civic and religious buildings in wood, almost nothing remains. The splendid Kyongju capital—square in plan, with high city walls pierced by twenty large gates, with its wide rectilinear streets laid out in a chessboard pattern, with fortress towers at each angle of the walls, and situated in a fertile valley—contained almost a million inhabitants. Its wooden buildings, together with its numerous religious complexes and palaces, were completely destroyed during the Japanese invasion of 1592-98. Nevertheless, the foundations of some buildings have come down to us, along with a number of tombs with tumuli in which precious funeral offerings have been found; the stone monuments that surrounded the royal tombs, graced by imposing figures of men and animals; the pagodas; the *pudo*; the lanterns of the religious complexes (often constructed in accordance with the twin-pagoda plan—two pagodas placed to the side of the façade of the main hall); and above all, the two temples of Pulguk-sa and Sokkulam, which confirm the level of maturity achieved by builders of the Silla Kingdom. Tradition tells us that both temples were ordered by the prime minister Kim Taisung, but while only the entrance stairs of the first complex remain, the balustrades, a few stone pagodas and lanterns—sufficient to indicate the scope of the grand style of the period—the cave temple of Sokkulam has survived almost intact. It is a singular example of its kind, first constructed with large square stones to create an artificial domed structure and then covered with earth. Its plan is a typical one that might be called an apse plan, consisting of a rotunda preceded by a rectangular access antechamber. As such, it is related on the one hand to primitive Indian plans for Buddhist rock constructions, and on the other to tombs of the Three Kingdoms period, especially by the two imposing octagonal pillars placed at the entrance to the rotunda. A colossal statue of Buddha at the center of the circular shrine, around which the faithful can perform the rite of *pradakshinā*, takes the place of the stupa of the Indian prototypes, while statues and reliefs of Buddhas and Bodhisattvas are harmoniously placed in niches or as panels along the walls of the two rooms.

Both at Pulguk-sa and Sokkulam, the imitation in stone of wooden structural elements is accomplished by preserving all the massive bulk of the material, without falling into the minute study of details that is found in some stone works of the Chinese T'ang dynasty. Since we so sorely lack evidence, we have no way of knowing whether or not there existed a typically Korean style in wooden architecture. But it would seem that such Japanese examples as the main hall of the Tōshōdaiji and the Hokkakudo of the Eizanji may in a certain way—in their simplicity of line and also in the essential nature of their structures—reflect the skill of Silla carpenters.

Koryo Kingdom (A.D. 918-1392)
It is said that the Koryo period represents the medieval phase of Korean civilization and that, at least until the twelfth century, what was taking place in the artistic field represented a late and provincial repetition of T'ang

structure constituted a model for constructions of the next period, like the other two more widespread types of stone structures, the *pudo* and the lantern. The first of these is a funerary monument for Buddhist monks, inspired by the stupa and consisting of a base, a pedestal, a central structure, and a roof with a high finial. The so-called lantern, which often assumes considerable proportions and is connected in front to a pagoda or to a principal religious hall, is similarly structured, despite infinite variations owing to the prevalence of one or another construction element—by a base, a pedestal in the form of a more or less slender pilaster, a central body, and a roof topped by a finial with several umbrellas.

examples. It seems more readily demonstrable that what took place in architecture was a coherent development from classical prototypes of the Silla period toward a greater decorative sensibility and a search for more fanciful forms, though these are always measured and contained. It is undeniable that the successive invasions of the Khitan (Liao dynasty), the Jurchen (Chin dynasty), and finally the Mongols (Yüan dynasty), together with the close ties between Korea and the Sung court, contributed to the formulation of new structural and stylistic conceptions and of new types of buildings. The octagonal pagoda of the Khitan and Jurchen was taken up, for example, in the nine-story pagoda of Wol-chong-sa at P'yong-ch'ang Kun

(eleventh century). The Indian style of wooden buildings, called in Korea *Chusimp'o*, is inspired by T'ien-chu, the so-called Indian style of southern China, especially in the forms it assumes in Fukien. It is probable that Mongol craftsmen had worked on the ten-story pagoda of Kyong-ch'on-sa in Seoul (A.D. 1348), a jewel of architectural and decorative forms. Unfortunately, only a very few examples of wooden architecture have come down to us. The splendid capital of Song-do (Kaesong), with its ample staircases, gardens, and palaces—which while respecting the requirements of the mountainous terrain, preserved an integrally balanced harmony of its own—has been totally destroyed by the continuous invasions. One might,

placed at intervals with measured potency; in the interiors, the usual coffered ceiling is replaced by beams of different dimensions and height supported by a system of brackets. The traditional style, called *Tap'o* or multibracket style, in which brackets are placed in an intermediate position between the columns, comes to be applied at this time with less frequency, however much constructions of the *Chusimp'o* kind, especially of the later period (the Tai-ung Chon of the Su-dok-sa at Yesan Kun, for example) have an increased number of bracket arms placed in the traditional position. Among stone constructions, pagodas of the Silla type become smaller, but accentuate their verticality through a greater number of stories and the changed proportion between the base and the body of the building.

The dimensions of the stone blocks with which they are constructed increase enormously, until each story comes to be constituted by a single monolith. Even the traditional shape is often modified, leading to pagodas that are polygonal in plan, or circular, like those of the so-called Hill of the Many Pagodas (Tat'ap Pong), which go back to the thirteenth century. The *pudo* and the "lanterns," in addition to their greater vertical thrust, also show considerable variety of form and shape; they may be cylindrical, bell-shaped, or polygonal. Often, they are covered with delicate ornamentation, like the lantern of the Silluk-sa at Yonju Kun (second half of the fourteenth century), or the *pudo* of the monk Hong-pob (1017) in the Kyong-bok at Seoul; with its spherical body and covering in the form of a mushroom, it is one of the most valid examples of the fantasy and creative power of Koryo architecture.

Li Dynasty (A.D. 1392-1910)

A particular phenomenon that in reality forms part of the tradition of Far Eastern architecture, but that is highly accentuated in this period, is the imitation of the antique, shared by the China of both the Ming and the Ch'ing. This is partly due to the importance given by the Li dynasty to a rigid application of Confucian doctrine, and thus to the cult of the past, in a vast area extending from political and social organization to art and culture. This, despite the fact that in an early period—that is, up until the Japanese invasion of 1592-98, which represents a historical gap not only politically but also artistically, because of the destruction of works of art and the disordering of the social fabric—palaces, temples, and fortifications preserve intact their great strength and majesty of line. Beginning in the late sixteenth century, these characteristics undergo a decline, and buildings show an exaggerated grandeur and an excessive elaboration of decoration, with lotus blossoms, peonies, geometric motifs, and densely intertwined vine tendrils, especially in the interiors. Another peculiar characteristic of the period, due in part to the diminished importance of Buddhism, is the gradual disappearance of ceremonial constructions in stone. In the fifteenth century, stone pagodas inspired by Koryo examples were still being built, like the ten-story pagoda of Won-gak-sa in Seoul (1468), which imitates the Kyong-ch'on-sa, or the more traditional one of Nak-san-sa at Yang-yang-kun

however, observe that in the Indian style—that is, in *Chusimp'o* works—the outlines of similar Chinese models are maintained, with the column assuming by itself the weight of the architrave and with brackets jutting perpendicularly to the façades that support the strong projection of the roof. In Korean works, however, the bracket system is never transformed into a complicated tangle of projecting members, as occurs in some Japanese buildings. Here structural tension is counterbalanced by bracket arms placed in the traditional position (parallel to the façade) and by the lesser height of the pillars.

In the oldest examples—the twelfth-thirteenth century Keung-nak Chon of the Pong-chong-sa at An-dong Kun, which for certain architectural details may be considered the archetype, and the slightly later Mu-ryang-su Chon of the Pu-sok-sa—the brackets and columns, set off against lighter walls, are

(late fifteenth century). Except for a few other rare instances, we no longer witness that repetition of votive monuments that, since the period of the Three Kingdoms, had constituted the characteristic element of religious complexes. What is preserved, on the other hand, are the traditional forms and structures of dynastic necropolises; the skill of Korean craftsmen in the use of stone is attested by numerous bridges with one or more finely worked spans, and by the massive vaults of "ice houses," used to preserve ice during the summer months. This period saw the flourishing of civic architectural structures in many materials—brick, stone blocks, wood. The colossal brick or stone fortifications surrounding the principal cities, which were often surmounted by wooden pavilions or roofs, definitely show close ties with similar Ming and Ch'ing constructions, but also demonstrate a sense of measure and rhythm that is typically Korean.

The city walls and gates of Suwon (1794-96), for whose construction tools introduced from Europe by way of China were used, are a typical example, as is the Nan-dai Mun, the principal gateway of Seoul, the southern one of 1448, and the much later eastern one of 1869. Both are remains of the monumental walls that surrounded the capital. Wooden architecture undergoes a new flowering of the *Chusimp'o* style up until the fifteenth century, as demonstrated by the classical proportions and measured harmony of the Hai-t'al Mun, the To-kab-sa at Yong-am Kun (middle of the fifteenth century), and of the Hall of Paradise (Keuk-nak Chon) of the Mu-wi-sa at Kang-jin-kun, which belongs to the same period. By the beginning of the sixteenth century, we find a revival of the traditional local style, the *Tap'o*, which in the seventeenth century will completely supplant the *Chusimp'o* style. An example from the period of transition between the two styles in the Myong-jong Mun of the Ch'ang-kyong: on the outside it shows a bracket system placed integrally with respect to the supporting columns, typical of the *Tap'o* style, and on the inside has an uncoffered ceiling, with the framework of roof and beams exposed in accordance with the *Chusimp'o*. After the Japanese invasion, the *Tap'o* style was to evolve toward greater decoration, such as can also be found in Chinese architecture of the time. The increased use of the *Shoi-so* (literally "ox tongue," so called for its elongated form) is proof of this tendency.

From their initial inconspicuous position as ornaments situated at each corner of the building (for example, in the Nan-dai Mun in Seoul), the *Shoi-so* become a recurrent decorative motif. They take the form of long curved hooks placed on the bracket arms, making the linear structure heavier and more complicated, as in the Tai-ung Chon (1765) of the old and renowned complex of Pulguk-sa. The development of the bracket structure toward a purely decorative form is even more obvious. In the so-called *Ik-kong*—a bracket system in which, with every supporting function lost, the brackets are reduced to a single richly decorated block—the search for ornamentation goes beyond all bounds, as in the Pang-hwa Su-ryu Chong at Suwon (1796). At the same time, both the shape and form of roofs become more complicated. To "T" and "L" shapes are added round and polygonal ones, while the roofs acquire more ridges and are adorned with acroteria in bronze, wood, or ceramic. Façades and interiors are decorated with luminous colors in a hitherto unknown search for chromatic effects. Such great complexes as the Kyong-bok and Ch'ang-dok, residential palaces in Seoul, whose splendid gardens are filled with pavilions of the most varied forms, are an example. Here the buildings blend marvelously with nature, and the intervention of man in the sphere of nature itself tends to be limited to the minimum necessary to preserve its genuine beauty. The two complexes are the most valid example of the remarkable aesthetic value inherent even in some of the latest works of Li architecture.

Modern Period (1910-   )

Korea was opened to modern Western technology under political pressure by Japan, which by the terms of the Treaty of Kang-kwa (February 27, 1876) forced the Li dynasty to open certain ports to foreign trade. In the long period of Japanese rule, from 1910 to 1945, not only were Western building types, forms, and techniques introduced, but systematic archaeological research and the scientific study of ancient traditional architecture were also begun, resulting in numerous excavation expeditions and the widespread restoration of monuments.

At the same time, however, the weight of Japanese rule suppressed, at least in part, any independent development in a modern direction and obstructed the emergence of a new national architecture. Attempts to exploit the past ignored its most vital aspects. Buildings were thus erected that were often the fruit of a Japanese (and not Korean) interpretation of Western trends. As such, the value of such structures is limited, and in any case they were the expression of a foreign taste. The broad urbanization policy that enlarged the principal cities was carried out in some cases in a disorganized and artificial manner.

Even during the later postwar period, political events made it impossible to achieve an organic formulation of a modern Korean architecture, despite the Koreans' enthusiasm for their regained independence and their re-evaluation of traditional values.

Only at present is the attempt being made (in a different manner in each of the two republics into which the peninsula is divided) to examine international techniques and adapt them to the traditional needs of the country. Some interesting results have been obtained, especially for the interiors and rooms of buildings. These may constitute a point of departure for future developments.

Paola Mortari Vergara Caffarelli

161

193. Circular and rectangular types
of pit dwellings, Jomon period (from
Tamburello, 1963).

194. Dwelling with floor sunk into
the earth, Yayoi period (from
Tamburello, 1963).

Prehistory and Protohistory

The most recent archaeological discoveries date the presence of man in the
Japanese islands from the Old Stone Age. The Paleolithic Japanese—in the
course of an uninterrupted cultural evolution that lasted for several hundred
thousand years, specifically until the Neolithic cultures emerged in the last
millennia before the Christian Era—never lived as troglodytes in caves or
rock shelters, but dwelt in the open on the slopes of mountains or on river
banks. We have no evidence to assist us in a reconstruction of their primitive
types of dwellings; we can, however, assume that they must have been
hidden in forests and thickets and covered with branches or animal skins.
An ancient Ainu legend speaks of a population in the archipelago known
as *koropok-guru*, a word signifying the inhabitants of underground dwellings.
We do not know precisely to which people the name refers, but it is
nevertheless significant that the earliest huts of which we have archaeological
evidence appear to have been sunk in the ground, with the floor dug to
a depth that varies between 16 and 40 inches. This type of pit dwelling
remains characteristic for a great part of the Neolithic period, and is
connected with a widespread prehistoric tradition of hut architecture for
cold climates in many northern regions of the Eurasian continent. Such huts,
square or circular in plan, usually measured some 13 to 20 feet in width.
Elevation was obtained by a wooden framework consisting of a number of
poles driven into the ground and crossing at the top. In those huts with a
square plan, a horizontal beam was employed for the whole length of the
hut and served to secure the crossed poles along the roof line. The structure
was covered with the branches and bark of trees, and was essentially a shed,
since the walls of the hut were to all intents and purposes constituted by
the sides of the pit.

In later Neolithic settlements—that is, until the middle of the first
millennium B.C.—types of huts appeared in which the floor was at ground
level. This innovation is surely due, at least in some regions, to milder
climatic conditions and may indicate a process of adaptation to the
environment. In any case, it marks the beginning of a true architectural
development; it was no longer a matter of extracting shelter from the earth,
but of constructing a building whose elevation was required not only to
support the roof but also to define the interior space or spaces by walls, even
though these were still covered by vegetable materials.

The next stage in this process is marked by the appearance, in the final
pre-Christian centuries, of new types of huts with floors raised on posts—that
is, with platforms elevated above ground level. This kind of architecture,
essentially of lake dwellers, was perhaps introduced into the Japanese islands
from southeastern Asia, along with agriculture and in particular the
cultivation of rice by irrigation. But not all of the old construction methods
were abandoned. That the use of a scissors crossing for the poles and a
horizontal beam for the roof was preserved can be deduced, for example,
from the long survival of these elements in Japanese architecture of the

195. Corridor of a funerary tumulus from the Kofun period: construction sketch (from Tamburello, 1963).

196. Small model of a house (haniwa) of the Kofun period, originally from the Prefecture of Gunma (Tokyo, National Museum).

historical era, still to be seen in modern replicas of such ancient Shinto shrines as Ise and Izumo. We must nevertheless keep in mind that such elements are very common in wooden architecture, and it is difficult to determine whether they are firmly connected with the architectural tradition already established in the islands in Neolithic times or with some other influence of foreign origin. In any case, the possibility of frequent encounters with the architecture of southern China, of Indochina, Indonesia, and in general with the island areas of the South Pacific exists. Such encounters are easy to explain when we remember that during the Bronze Age the growth of settled agricultural civilization, under the preponderant influence of the Chinese, provided these regions with common economic and social foundations.

The fact that, as a result of an entirely new cultural influx, Japan should have adopted a typically southern architecture in the first centuries of the Christian Era—which was not relinquished despite many disadvantages owing to the environmental and climatic conditions of much of the archipelago—reveals the importance and scope of the new cultural inheritance of the Bronze Age. Various factors favored the choice and spread of light and open building structures in preference to the more solid and enclosed ones suitable to a continental climate. The first is that a tradition of southern life established itself from the beginning in the subtropical area of the southern Japanese islands and from there was gradually carried toward the central ones. A second factor is that the northern part of the archipelago had scant influence on the development of Japan's culture and long remained an area for colonization, prone to submit to external pressures rather than offer alternatives even in the sphere of architecture. Only certain types of fortification structures may reveal a northern inspiration. Japanese architecture has invariably remained, for all of its history, a southern architecture; whatever technical and structural improvements have been accepted in the course of centuries—even as regards the positioning and adaptation of the building structure—have done nothing to alter this basic characteristic. The predominant use of wood was encouraged by ample forests, and this contributed to the development and perfection of techniques for utilizing its natural qualities (for absorbing humidity from the air and restoring it to dryness). Such observations on the part of the Japanese discouraged the use of paints or varnishes, or the covering of wooden surfaces with waterproof materials. This led to the habit of leaving every structural element exposed, and of maintaining a raw appearance, the most natural one possible, for the architectural work.

Asuka Period (A.D. 552-645)

The Chinese influence in the historical era, penetrating Japan first by way of Korea, brought the introduction of new architectural structures and techniques, new ways of arranging building areas, and principles for urban planning. Buddhism introduced new types of religious architecture of a

monumental kind that had already been known to China for at least three centuries. There also appeared a new residential type of architecture, which must have been sponsored and built by a good number of the more than one hundred thousand immigrants from Korea and Manchuria who at this time were settling in the Japanese islands.

Unfortunately, there is little remaining evidence of such works. Recent archaeological discoveries have brought to light the foundations of the city that after the fourth century A.D. served as the capital of the first Japanese state body. Official historical tradition speaks of the palaces built by the sovereigns Ojin and Nintoku from the fourth to fifth centuries A.D. in Naniwa, on the outskirts of present-day Osaka. Later, some imperial residences were erected in the area of Asuka and Fujiwara, in the vicinity of modern Nara. An age-old custom of Japanese political life allowed each sovereign on his accession to the throne to establish in a chosen place the seat of his own residence, where a palace was built that could later be moved to, or reconstructed in, other localities in the event that particular circumstances required it. The custom hardly indicates an attitude of permanence, and may perhaps be related to the Japanese nation's unification and political organization by a class of warrior knights with nomadic traditions who came from the outlying steppes of Central Asia and established themselves in the archipelago about the fourth century A.D. A seminomadic tradition, or at least one not rigidly sedentary, has moreover remained characteristic of the whole of Japanese history. The house, which is not at all conceived to last for centuries, and its scant furnishings are almost symbolic of an atavistic reminiscence of life in a tent, where one is subject to all the shifts and changes of the natural condition. To this may be added the characteristics of the Japanese islands—the frequent earthquakes, hurricanes, and fires, all of which have combined to increase a sense of precariousness and instability.

At least a partial consequence of the frequent transfer of the imperial residence was the lack of any notable urban development, or in any case until the remodeling of government institutions along the lines of imperial China required the construction of a permanent capital. Nevertheless, Asuka had already been laid out between the sixth and eighth centuries, and with its numerous public and residential buildings, Shinto shrines, and Buddhist temples, had the appearance of a capital.

The support of Buddhism granted by Shōtoky as emperor (A.D. 593-621) had made it possible to construct the first temples at the expense of the treasury. The oldest monumental complex for which we have the best documentation is the Hōryūji in the vicinity of Nara; its original nucleus goes back to the seventh century. The monastery consists of a large quadrangular cloister, with its principal entrance gate to the south, enclosing a broad open area within which rises a five-story pagoda and a low pavilion. The latter contained the chief iconostasis of the cult; a building for the reading of sacred texts is situated behind it, flanked by lesser structures for the library and the temple bell. The cloister has a projecting roof and four intercolumniar spaces on its façade—the two center ones for passage, and those to the sides to hold statues of the "protector kings." The Golden Hall, rectangular in plan, rises on a stone platform with twenty-eight pilasters that support the upper part of the structure with its curved eaves and form four spans on one side and five on the other. The columns show a slight entasis remotely derived from the West, to which even the low stone stylobates are related. The function of the capitals, on the other hand, is replaced by a system of bracket arms connected by horizontal beams. The pagoda—which is the symbolic equivalent of the stupa, or Buddhist shrine generically inspired by the funerary tumulus—is developed on a square plan, with a central pilaster that ends at the top in a series of bronze rings symbolizing the parasols of Indian stupas. The stories are of decreasing size, the four lower ones with three trusses on each side, the fifth with two trusses; the roofing has curved eaves, as in the other buildings. The pagoda is certainly the most characteristic and most successful structure in Buddhist architecture, and the one to achieve the greatest vertical elevation and number of stories. Intended in its capacity as a shrine to be a closed structure, it remained exempt from any need to articulate its interior spaces, and thus its organic composition is wholly external. In Japanese architecture, it is

perhaps only the pagoda that obeys standards of monumentality wherein the aesthetic is divorced from the functional. But in so doing it also represented the limit, and an obstacle to the stylistic development of this type of building, which rarely departed from the traditional pattern of construction.

Nara Period (A.D. 645-784)

Heijōkyō, modern-day Nara, was founded in 710 as the first permanent capital of the state. Its rectangular plan, the chessboard layout of the streets, the removal of the imperial court and government buildings to the north-central sector of the city were all elements modeled after Changan, the Chinese capital of the Sui and T'ang dynasties. The architecture, too, follows the plans and forms of Chinese buildings, and the T'ang palace was the prototype of the new courtly residences. A complex of buildings was distributed symmetrically at the cardinal points around a central area designated as a garden. The main building, which housed the head of the family, was oriented to the south and connected to the lesser buildings by covered verandas.

Within a few years, the new metropolis had become an important Buddhist center; many monasteries were transferred there and other new ones built. Between 755 and 770 construction was begun on the Tōshōdaiji, founded by Chien-chên (Ganjin, 688-763), who had been summoned to Japan from China to re-establish the rules for correct monastic discipline. The temple offers a synthesis of Chinese and Japanese structural and stylistic elements, and also represents a free translation of continental models from stone into wood. Structures were more simple and proportioned, but nevertheless still tended toward a grandeur produced by rather rigid and heavy forms. The original buildings of the Tōshōdaiji were perhaps the reading hall and the Golden Hall. The first, we are told, had been built as a pavilion of the imperial palace of Heijōkyō and was later turned over to the temple. The tradition is suggestive of the ties between religious and residential architecture.The Golden Hall, which unfolds on a plan of seven intercolumniations by four, likewise perpetuates in all probability the example of Chinese T'ang palaces.

The most grandiose architectural achievement of the Nara period was the Tōdaiji, the "Great Eastern Temple," the first Buddhist religious center built wholly at the expense of the treasury, by the wish of the emperor Shōmu (A.D. 701-756), who in 741 also decreed that a monastery for men and a convent for women be erected in every province of the country at state expense. In the construction of the Tōdaiji, it was ensured that each building of the cult should constitute a complex in itself and be built within a cloister.

Heian Period (A.D. 784-1185)

The network of temples officially built for the protection of the country provided an impetus for the development of architecture, the arts, and

197, 198. Small model of a house of the Kofun period, originally from the Prefecture of Gunma (Tokyo, National Museum).

199. Nara, Tōshōdaiji.

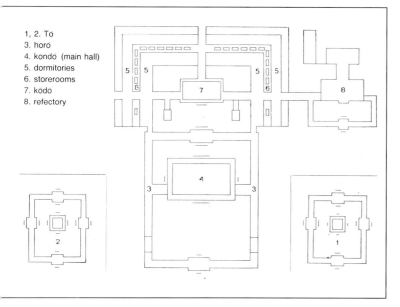

1, 2. To
3. horo
4. kondō (main hall)
5. dormitories
6. storerooms
7. kodo
8. refectory

culture in general. At the same time, however, they signaled a pervasive penetration by Buddhism into every sector of Japan's public and political life that ended with a massive interference by the clergy in affairs of state. To escape from the influence of Buddhism, the emperor Kwammu, who ruled from 782 to 805, decided in 784 to transfer his residence to Nagaoka, where the work of building a new capital was immediately begun. When a series of calamities and unlucky circumstances in 793 discouraged progress on this selected site, a new location was chosen in the region of Yamashiro. There, in the following year, the first foundations of Heian-kyo were laid, the city that was later to be known by the name of Miyako or Kyoto and which remained the imperial residence until 1869.

Kyoto was situated in the center of the country, a better geographical position than that of Nara, which was surrounded by mountains and rather isolated and difficult to reach. Furthermore, Kyoto was linked to the coast by the Kamo River, which emptied into the Yodo and thus constituted a line of communication with Osaka, already the chief commercial port of the Japanese archipelago. The layout of the city did not differ from that of Nara, or in the final analysis from that of Changan. A rectangular area of about 3.1 by 2.8 miles, with the lesser sides to the north and south, was crisscrossed by wide parallel and perpendicular streets. A wall with a double moat enclosed the perimeter of the urban center, on whose northern side rose the imperial palace with a complex of residences and offices occupying in all an area of about 1,800 square yards. In addition to its greater dimensions,

the new capital differed from Nara in the character of its architecture; Kyoto's palaces, temples, and private dwellings employed the first truly original Japanese results. The buildings, while still inspired by Chinese models, were marked by local taste and by suggestions of the already operative admixtures of Buddhist architecture. Materials, structures, and construction methods increasingly recalled the ancient traditions of the Japanese islands. The use of wooden and brick roofing tiles was combined with coverings of tree bark and rice thatch; wall elements in mortar, stone, and clay were abandoned for exclusively wooden structures. The buildings of the imperial palace, for example, were planned in a pure Japanese style, and constructed in simple wood with plank floors and partitions; and the roofs were covered with the bark of the *hinoki*, a variety of cypress.

The notable dimensions of the buildings involved a series of technical solutions definitely stemming from Japanese architecture. Pilasters were established as the main supporting structures, and thus the walls were conceived merely as curtains extending among the various supports to allow for the articulation of interior spaces. The basic unit of measurement was the *ken*, which indicated the distance between two pilasters and might vary from approximately 10 feet to 6. Some buildings of the imperial palace, for example the Shishinden, set forth the lines of what was later to become the typical aristocratic residence (*shindenzukuri*). According to this style, which had already appeared under Chinese influence during the previous Nara period, buildings were placed symmetrically on two arms that defined a broad inner area as a garden. In the garden, there was usually a lake, from whose waters emerged rocks that symbolized islands, connected to each other and to the shore by small stone or wooden bridges. The *Sakuteiki*, a thirteenth-century manual on the art of gardening, describes this style of garden in minute detail. Its miniaturist criteria were intended to harmonize the architecture with the landscape, blending in a single expression the work of nature and that of man through a combination of two distinct orders of compositional elements—one vegetable (flowers, small trees, shrubs), the other tectonic (hills, rocks, ponds, streams). By a careful attention to proportions, the spatial effects of nature were to be kept intact.

Among the few surviving examples of Heian residential architecture, albeit from the end of the period, we may note the Byōdōin, whose *Hoōdō*, or "phoenix hall" (from the gilded bronze phoenix that surmounts one of its structures), is the only original complex and one of the most elegant and refined works in all of Japanese architecture. The pavilion, built in the eleventh century, is formed by a series of structures with halls and side galleries that on different levels face the shores of a lake. The interior spaces are richly decorated with polychrome lacquer, inlays of mother-of-pearl, applications of gilded copper, and painted coffering. A lavish taste for ornament is also displayed in the decoration of the internal structural elements of Buddhist temples. Brackets and beams are lacquered or covered by thin metal sheets, and the ends decorated with openwork, as in the

202. Nara, Tōdaiji, hall of the
Great Buddha, interior, detail
of crossbeams.

Golden Hall of the Chūsonji temple, from the first half of the twelfth century, and also the Jingoji in Kyoto.

The esoteric Buddhist doctrines of Tendai and Shingon, transplanted at this time to the Japanese islands, revived the fervor of the primitive Buddhist communities, cultivating ideals of mysticism and the hermit's life that in turn encouraged the construction of monasteries in the solitude of the mountains. The abandonment of level urban areas for the rocky slopes of mountains brought numerous innovations to Buddhist architecture. Strict standards of symmetry in the disposition of buildings were given up, and structures were lightened and reduced in size. This general structural and stylistic reconsideration led to the search for a more organic adaptation of the architectural work to the surrounding landscape. Kōngobuji and Enryakuji were the two most important mountain monasteries of the period and served as models for later ones. Their buildings, scattered through the forest, literally merged with nature, while borrowing a traditional simplicity from Shinto architecture.

This was the moment of return for an influence that hitherto had been exercised in only one direction—by Buddhist on Shinto architecture. Shinto-Buddhist religious syncretism now encouraged a mixture of architectural forms and elements, for the most part decorative ones, like the metal trimmings that had been completely unknown to more ancient Shinto structures. On the whole, however, the original characteristics of the architecture of the islands were not lost—the austere simplicity of form and essentially linear conception of each level of the building, with scant structural differences even in their stylistic variations. Diverse styles were distinguished more than anything by the disposition of colonnades, the incline and projection of roofs, and the removal of entrance structures to the shorter or longer sides of the building, parallel or orthogonal in relation to the roof line. The wood, originally left in its unfinished state, was now customarily painted, in red or cinnabar, as in Buddhist temples; the roof beams and hips were curved; and the eaves, supported by brackets, became increasingly complex and elaborate.

The brackets, placed between pillars and architraves to diminish the opening of the latter and ensure an effective system of support, constituted perhaps the most notable structural element introduced from the architecture of the continent, allowing an equilibrium of forces between horizontal planes and vertical structures, as well as a greater load capacity on the pillars. Various types were employed, in accordance with numerous systems, and combined in a more or less composite fashion—projecting, hanging, etc.—but the usual bracket was boat-shaped (called *funa-hijiki* in Japanese), and connected to the pillars by means of intermediate structures that took the place of capitals and normally consisted of square blocks. In more complex forms, the use of brackets was extended not only longitudinally and sideways but also vertically, and gave way to an increased number of orders corresponding to the various levels that served to support intermedi-

203. *Nara, Tōdaiji,* nandaimon
(southern portal).

204. *Nara (outskirts), Hōryūji, plan of the central complex: a) original disposition of the buildings; b) present disposition; c) transverse section of the kondō. (from Ritti, 1963).*

206. *Nara, Yakushiji, plan (from Ritti, 1963).*

207. *Nara, Yakushiji, eastern pagoda.*

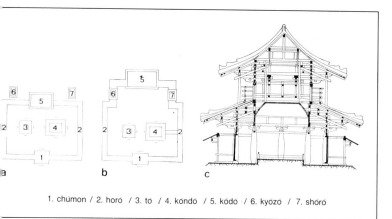

1. chūmon / 2. horō / 3. tō / 4. kondō / 5. kōdō / 6. kyōzō / 7. shōrō

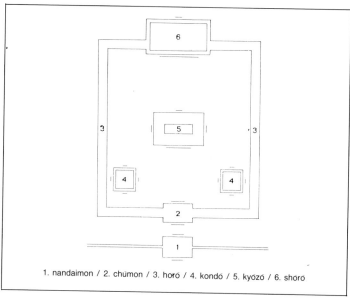

1. nandaimon / 2. chūmon / 3. horō / 4. kondō / 5. kyōzō / 6. shōrō

205. *Nara (outskirts), Hōryūji, kondō, exterior.*

ate reinforcing beams. First used in Buddhist architecture, they were later adopted in residential buildings, and finally in Shinto shrines at the time when a number of technical innovations were being introduced in the latter during the Heian period.

The Hachiman sanctuary at Tsurugaoka, which goes back to the twelfth century, is one of the most characteristic examples of architectural commingling, with its high canopy roofs and playfully curved structures that form the central entablatures of certain buildings. It represents, moreover, one of the more standardized types of late Shinto architecture, and together with *nagare*, *kasuga*, and *hie* models, figures among the principal styles followed by later shrines, which rarely carried out new stylistic experiments. The Hachiman shrine was composed of two groups of buildings joined by a structure in the middle. A double entrance was placed on the sides parallel to the roof line. Even in their general composition, the structure of new Shinto sanctuaries, as compared to the more ancient places of worship, was modified. The number of auxiliary buildings was increased, as well as their size, while even Buddhist pagodas and pavilions were erected within the same enclosures.

Kamakura Period (A.D. 1185-1333)

The establishment of the Kamakura shogunate, which transferred the powers of the state from the hands of the imperial court to those of a military class, had profound effects on the arts and culture of Japan. A general

sobriety asserted itself in architecture, leading to a preference for simple, unadorned structures. New residences heralded the "warrior style" (*buke-zukuri*), in which buildings were surrounded by narrow moats or stockades. Buildings were no longer distributed around a garden but preferably grouped in a single body under the same roof, or a group of adjoining roofs, so as to ensure better defense. The old gardens were replaced by training grounds.

Even Buddhist religious architecture underwent numerous modifications. Two new styles were imported from the continent: the Indian style (*Tenjikuyō*)—introduced, however, from southern China; and the Chinese style (*Karayō*), so called to distinguish it from the *Wayō*, which by now had become the national style in the Japanese islands. Many temples were destroyed during the civil wars that broke out at the close of the Heian period; they were now rebuilt in the *Tenjikuyō* style. This was the case of Tōdaiji, for whose reconstruction absolutely new structures were employed, such as the *nandaimon*, or southern portal, which sums up the technical characteristics of the *Tenjikuyō* style by the use of large beams placed for the most part in a rigidly orthogonal manner. A greater vertical development of buildings was obtained by an increased number of bracket orders, which were often of only two arms, placed perpendicular and parallel to the walls, and these were inserted directly into the trunk of the pillar with no intermediate block. Roofs were frequently of a double order, in typical pavilion form and covered with tiles.

Some characteristics of *Tenjikuyō* architecture were common to *Karayō*, such as the structural elements of the brackets, roof tiles, and roofs, which in this unifying sense represented the result of a Chinese architectural tradition. The *Karayō* style was nevertheless distinguished by the layout of the monasteries, which were going back to the old rectangular plan with its symmetrical disposition of the major buildings, placed chiefly along the central axis. Applied to Chinese Ch'an (Zen) temples of the Southern Sung dynasty, the new style was introduced into Japan by the monk Eisai (1141-1215), and was first used in 1202 in the construction of the Kenninji monastery in Kyoto. It was later employed for the five great Zen monasteries of Kamakura.

Engakuji, dating from the thirteenth century, is considered one of the purest examples of the *Karayō* style. The *Shariden*, or hall of relics, is the main building of the temple. The portico displays the typical yoke arch; the wood, left in its natural color, bears some sculptural decoration, which softens the solidity and linearity of the architectural structure. Moreover, the building represents a new interpretation of the reliquary shrine, hitherto constituted by the pagoda. The pagoda now begins to decline in importance, and while it does not actually disappear, it is erected outside the main enclosure. The meditative and contemplative doctrine of Zen gave precedence to other structures within the central enclosure. These might be the meditation hall, or even the garden, conceived so as to dissolve the

architectural work in the landscape, in a setting that helps to coordinate the lines and proportions of the buildings in accordance with standards of sobriety that annul any monumental effect.

Muromachi Period (A.D. 1333-1573)

The warrior spirit and the austere ideals of Zen encouraged a simplicity of life and customs that spread widely throughout the provinces of the archipelago, and architecture conformed to this orientation. But things soon began to change in the surroundings of the capitals of Kyoto and Kamakura. Along with Zen, the new art of the Yüan and Ming dynasties had been imported from China, producing a decided tendency toward decoration and a taste for ostentation and luxury. When the old shogun seat of Kamakura was abandoned and the new Ashikaga shogunate was established in the Muromachi quarter of Kyoto, the distances between the military aristocracy and the court nobility were once again reduced. Rivalry and exhibitionism at the upper levels of society led to a profuse indulgence, as a show of wealth, in gold and bright color for the interiors of sumptuous dwellings, in their furnishings, wall paintings, and screens. Residential architecture particularly abounded in sculptural ornamentation and gilt decoration, while new stylistic solutions were sought in order to adapt the rigid *buke-zukuri* to the *shinden* style of ancient aristocratic houses.

One of the best works of the period is the Kinkakuji, a three-story building from the end of the fourteenth century. Its wide verandas are decorated in a lacquer and gold-leaf pattern that makes a striking contrast with the slender simplicity of the structures, and with the austere bark covering of the broad roofs of the second and top stories. Another example of such architecture, of an overall refinement in composition despite the sumptuousness of the decorative materials, is the Ginkakuji, or silver pavilion, built in the first half of the fifteenth century for a sophisticated circle of artists and monks.

The tea ceremony (*cha-no-yu*), introduced by the Zen masters, pointed the way for the planning of new buildings and acted to mitigate the tendency toward ostentation. The *cha-seki* and *cha-shitsu* (respectively, the tea hall and tea pavilion) were structures that contributed to the formulation of a new conception of residential architecture. The unadorned simplicity and modest dimensions suggested lighter and more intimate types of buildings, with slender rafters and pillars and with broad open surfaces on the outer walls achieved by means of sliding structures (*shōji*). Similarly, a more organic dispersal of buildings in the landscape was sought, and this also had a profound effect on the art of the garden. The classical elements of the *shinden* garden—its lakes, islands, and bridges—were no longer distributed so as to create a static scene, but rather a panorama that could be viewed from different observation points, as from pavilions scattered along the shores of lakes. Moreover, gardens adopted the symbolism characteristic of Zen, replacing, for example, water with sand to create the dry garden, an area

209. Nikko, Tōshōgū, Yōmei-mon *(Portal of Sunlight).*
210. *Kyoto, Nishi Honganji, the Hyunkaku, exterior.*
211. *Himeji, view of the castle.*

175

of terrain covered with white sand or with gravel, in which a succession of flagstones might symbolize a ford, or rocks stand for islands emerging from water. A typical example of this style is the Ryōanji garden in Kyoto, dating from the second half of the fifteenth century.

Momoyama Period (A.D. 1573-1614)

The first Europeans landed in the Japanese islands in 1542, and in no time the influence of the West was apparent, even in architecture. The warlike atmosphere of previous periods had already produced a fortress architecture in Japan. The introduction of firearms imposed new conceptions of defense, and in various localities castles and forts were built that were inspired as well by elements of the corresponding architecture of Europe. Fortresses, which had hitherto preferably been built in elevated positions, were now constructed on level ground and took on greater dimensions, with thicker walls, deeper moats, and high towers. Groups of buildings with an increased number of stories and diminishing roof orders were erected in wood, and reinforced by masonry on massive stone foundations in the form of a truncated pyramid. Among the more spectacular examples are the castles of Matsumoto, Kumamoto, and the "White Heron" of Himeji, with its four towers joined by narrow passages with turrets. The work, in stone and masonry, is also striking for certain minor innovations, such as the windows of the gratings, with small columns with or without capitals, and the open wall embrasures whose forms reflect the corresponding structures of Western castles.

Almost immediately, these architectural hybrids were to undergo—owing to the lack not only of a local architectural tradition but also of any tradition of castle life—a realignment with classical palace architecture. The most eloquent example of this process is seen in the Nijō castle, built in Kyoto in 1602 and remodeled in 1626. In slightly more than twenty years the original construction was radically altered. The three wall and moat enclosures designating the three fortresses, one inside the other, were kept. The feudal lord's residence—a complex of buildings grouped around a high central tower—was habitually erected in the inner enclosure (*honmaru*). But the castle lost its original compact appearance, and its buildings were separated and distributed over a vast area, part of which was assigned to gardens. The functionalism of fortified structures was replaced by a monumentality that was still in the Chinese taste, and the sense of solidity was expressed only symbolically by the heavy entablatures and roof gables, elaborately decorated with wooden and metal arabesques, openwork, and carving.

The merging of castle and classical palace architecture found its practical fulfillment in such cities as Kyoto, where the whole architectural tradition pointed in this direction.

Elsewhere, in more provincial or peripheral areas, castles represented an isolated phenomenon, almost devoid of consequences. Nevertheless,

their importance remained decisive, not for a renewal of architecture but for the urban development that they brought to the country, since it was around them that cities emerged and grew.

Yedo (Tokugawa) Period (A.D. 1615-1867)

The most imposing fort in the country was the castle of Yedo, which became the seat of the Tokugawa shogunate. The feudal lords, or *daimyos*, summoned to collaborate with the government built their residences withing its moats and broad bastions. Around this grandiose complex a city grew up, part of modern Tokyo; in a century it became the largest in the country. Not only did it represent the center of the state administration, but the actual heart of the nation, from which a network of roads and canals ensured communication with the most remote castle-cities of the *daimyos*. The exceptional growth experienced by urban centers at this time—one might say that hitherto Japan had known only capital cities and commercial ports—promoted building activity in all areas of the country. When we remember that Yedo alone reached a total of more than one million inhabitants in 1700, it is not hard to imagine the innovations introduced, especially in residential architecture. First of all, the scarcity of building sites required an ever more frequent elevation of two stories. Houses were habitually erected on raised stone platforms, 28 to 40 inches in height, on which rested the wooden flooring and pilasters that together with the horizontal beams formed the framework of the structure. Outer walls were now constructed with increasing frequency in masonry and plaster, at least on two sides; on the others, mobile partitions (*shōji*) were applied, or ample windows opening on verandas (*shoin*). The roof, always reinforced by wooden beams, was now commonly covered with tiles. The interior was divided into several rooms

214. Types of Shinto shrines. Left to right: façades, side views, and ground plans.

215. Kyoto, aerial view of the old imperial palace.
216. Osaka, Shitennōji, plan (from Ritti, 1963).

217. Kyoto, Ryōanji, detail of the stone and sand garden.

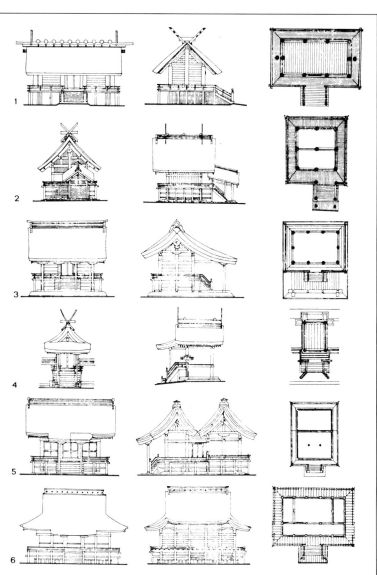

1. shinmei (shrine of Ise) / 2. taisha (shrine of Izumo) / 3. nagare (shrine of Kamo in Kyōto) / 4. kasuga (Kasuga shrine in Nara) / 5. hachiman (Usa-Hachiman shrine in Oita) / 6. hie (Hie shrine in Shiga) (from Ota, 1966).

by means of sliding walls (*fusuma*) and screens (*byōbu*), thus providing maximum flexibility of living quarters.

The increasingly widespread use of floor mats (*tatami*), whose dimensions were fixed at 32.94 by 72.32 inches, required new measurement units for the placing of pilasters; these could not be calculated as formerly on the basis of the distance between the centers of the pilasters, but in terms of the real space between one pilaster and another, taking into consideration the variations in their diameter. Greater freedom in planning, primarily for the distribution of rooms, was obtained by removing the supporting structures to the more external points of the building, especially to the corners, in such a way as to leave the interior spaces as free and uncluttered as possible. This resulted in a more complex scaffolding for roofs, so as to make up for the lack of supporting structures at the central points. In addition to the frequency of earthquakes and fires, this was one more reason why a limit was imposed to vertical elevation, which had recently been fixed at 101.7 feet for monumental buildings, as opposed to the approximately 312 feet once reached by the Tōdaiji pagoda.

The essential lines of Yedo civil architecture produced the so-called *sukiya* style, with which the development of Japanese residential architecture reaches its peak, establishing the type of dwelling to which the everyday house in the traditional style has remained firmly attached. The architectural masterpieces of the period, the Shūgakuin and Katsura villas—built in isolated settings in the environs of Kyoto during the first half of the seventeenth century—foreshadowed the transition from the *shoin* style to the *sukiya* by their deliberate search for suggestive spatial effects, their sense of measure and proportion, their position in a surrounding garden, and their simplicity of line and decor, as shown also by their use of wood left in its natural state. As for the monumental architecture of the period—omitting from our discussion the temples, which are generally modest and unadorned—it is best displayed in such mausoleum shrines as the renowed Tōshōgū at Nikko. Built in accordance with hybrid Shinto-Buddhist forms, these new complexes welcomed numerous Chinese influences, especially in the structure of their masonry arcades, and perhaps European ones as well in their internal twin vaults and columns with convex fluting. Ultimately, however, they constitute a phase of degeneration in Japanese architecture, perpetuating for a time a monumental conception that was a direct continuation of the castles and palaces of the Nijō type.

Modern Period (1868-   )

The Meiji restoration that began in 1868 transformed Japan politically and economically into a modern nation that more and more looked toward the West for inspiration. Among the many new programs undertaken, those relating to urban building and development were given a certain precedence. Traditional systems of wood construction were abandoned, since—especially for public utility works—they no longer corresponded to current

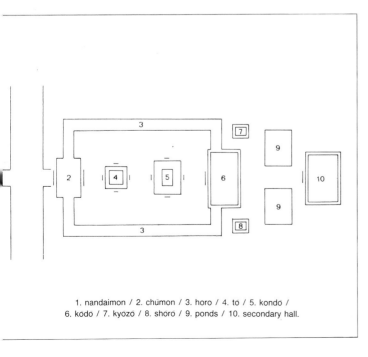

1. nandaimon / 2. chūmon / 3. horo / 4. tō / 5. kondō /
6. kōdō / 7. kyozō / 8. shōrō / 9. ponds / 10. secondary hall.

179

XXIII. Kyoto, Ryoanji, detail of the stone and sand garden.

XXIV. Kyoto, Kinkakiyi, (Temple of the Golden Pavilion).

needs. Attention was directed to techniques of Western architecture and building systems of the colonial type, which meanwhile had been developed and were spreading in the maritime cities of the archipelago as a result of the establishment of the first European and American settlements. Many of the new constructions consisted at first of buildings in a Westernizing style, whose wooden frameworks and structures were externally covered in stone or stucco. Among the first local architects to specialize in these new building techniques were Tadahiro Hayashi and Kisuke Shimizu II, both of whom were initiated into Western architectural methods through construction work at the foreign settlement of Yokohama. One of Shimizu's works was the famous Tsukiji Hotel in Tokyo, built in 1867-68 in a style that, though derived from the West, nevertheless preserves some traditional elements of native architecture.

Beginning in 1870, many European and American architects arrived in the principal cities of Japan. Together with other exponents of Western culture and on the invitation of the Japanese Government, they set in motion a program of modernization to which they themselves contributed greatly, by their own work and also by teaching in the universities that were founded

during the same years. They included the Englishmen T.J. Waters and Josiah Conder, the American R.P. Bridgens, the Frenchman C. de Boinville, the Italian C.V. Cappelletti, and the German H. Ende. Under their guidance, numerous public buildings were planned and executed in the varying historical styles of nineteenth-century Western architecture: Renaissance and Neoclassical, Romanesque and Gothic. Celebrated works of this period are the Mint in Osaka, built by Waters; the Shinbashi railway station, designed by Bridgens; the Historical Museum of Tokyo by Cappelletti; and the Nicholai Cathedral by Conder. These were for the most part imposing two or three-story constructions, massive in form, which in their meeting and mingling of different styles reflected the late nineteenth-century atmosphere of ferment in European architecture.

It was in this climate and with this formal eclecticism that the first Japanese architects trained by their Western counterparts (through courses in architecture and civil engineering inaugurated in 1875 at the College of Technology of the Imperial University in Tokyo) began to produce works. Among the first were Kingo Tatsuno, Tōyū Katayama, Yoriki Tsumaki, Yuzuru Watanabe, and Tamisuke Yokogawa. The considerable achieve-

ments of some of these architects—in Tokyo alone—included the stone and brick Bank of Japan building, built by Kingo Tatsuno in 1890-96; the Akasaka Palace, finished in 1909 after designs by Tōyū Katayama; the National Museum, built in 1908 by the same architect; the Central Station, of steel and brick, built in 1914 by Kingo Tatsuno; and the Imperial Theater of 1911 by Tamisuke Yokogawa. From the work of these first Japanese architects, building activity passed gradually into the hands of local designers and skilled workers, and a slow process of re-examining the values of traditional architecture began. The introduction in 1887 of a course in the history of architecture at the Imperial University must surely have helped to call attention to the values of the tradition, and to disseminate the first theories whereby the old might be fused with the new and the classical forms of Japanese architecture adapted to modern construction techniques.

The early decades of the twentieth century saw the appearance in Tokyo and other cities of the first constructions in reinforced concrete; their number was to grow following the disastrous earthquake of 1923. As a result of the construction materials employed for protection against earthquakes, buildings took on a certain heaviness of form and a massive solidity of structure. Nevertheless, new construction methods were soon adopted, in which there was a tendency to reduce wall structures as much as possible by the use of reinforced concrete pillars and wide glass windows.

Meanwhile, there was a notable influx of ideas from the new rationalistic European theories—to which Shinichirō Okada and Riki Sano were among the first to adhere—which championed an architectural dynamic to be achieved on the formal level by the geometric placing of volumes. The International Style, which thus seemed capable of development, was overwhelmed, however, upon the emergence of the Bunriha Kenchiku group, which, inspired by the Viennese Secession of the early twentieth century, welcomed to its ranks a large number of architects—among them Kikuji Ishimoto, Sutemi Horiguchi, and Mayumi Takizawa—who proposed the birth of a "new architecture." Their activities, which bore results in the 1920s, received support and corroboration from the work of Frank Lloyd Wright; the latter, with his naturalistic theories, had the opportunity to indicate during his stay in Japan for the construction of the Imperial Hotel in Tokyo the direction in which the new architecture should proceed. On the other hand, close contact with such famous architects as Le Corbusier,

Walter Gropius, and Ludwig Mies van der Rohe facilitated an evaluation of the functional and artistic needs to which the architectural work ought to respond. The failure of the rationalistic approach was due to the inevitable lack of spiritual and psychological sympathy for imported forms, and a solution was then sought in the reacquisition of the fundamental principles of traditional Japanese architecture: the articulation of space, harmony and rhythm of composition, fluency of volumes, luminosity and color. The German architect Bruno Taut and the Japanese Sutemi Horiguchi were important figures in this new orientation toward classical and traditional values. Interesting results were obtained by the readoption of classical stylistic models, as adapted to constructions that were very modern technically, and in which formerly wooden structures were replaced by metal. The principal buildings constructed in Tokyo during this period were the Kabuki Theater by Okada in 1922, the Imperial University's Institute of Technology by Uchida in 1923, and the University Library in 1925, designed by the same architect.

Meanwhile, a clear separation had emerged between the theoretical formulations of avant-garde architecture and the practical results achieved. Except for a very few works built in accordance with the new criteria, construction for the most part followed strictly functional forms, since the progressive extension of urban centers had produced a growing need for houses and public buildings. Domestic architecture, however, continued in its traditional ways, with small wooden constructions, usually of a single story. The question was raised as to whether the new principles of modern architecture might not be applied on a wider scale, and the work of Horiguchi, Hideto Kishida, Kunio Maekawa, and other architects led to the formation of the Nihon Kōsaky Bunka Remmei movement; among its chief objectives was the concrete realization of the new theories.

The major works of the 1930s include the central post offices in Tokyo and Osaka, designed by Tetsuo Yoshida; the large Sōgo department store in Osaka, designed by T. Murano; and the hospital for postal-telegraph workers built in Tokyo by Mamoru Yamada. They were for the most part constructed of reinforced concrete, with large windows, and broad verandas or projecting penthouses at the sides that at times resolved their heaviness of structure in dynamic perspective. These and other architectural works marked a definite orientation toward the new tendencies of modern architecture. The political atmosphere, however, soon made such a program unfeasible. Official architecture, under the banner of the now prevailing nationalism, turned back to a massive solidity of form and a static juxtaposition of structures that expressed the rigid, martial exterior imposed by the new artistic directives of the government. A classic example of this kind of architecture is the solemn and imposing Army Palace in Tokyo.

With the end of World War II, and as a result of the almost total destruction of many cities, the problem of rebuilding came urgently to the fore. But since the work of reconstruction had first to confront the more impelling needs, whole quarters of cities—largely composed of traditional wooden buildings or small masonry houses—were rebuilt without any preconceived plans. The difficulties of an organic and radical urban plan turned out to be insurmountable. A compromise solution was attempted by laying out new peripheral neighborhoods, built according to modern urban conceptions of autonomous centers and satellite cities. Official as well as residential architecture definitely adopted the new construction techniques and materials of reinforced concrete, as well as an ample employment of metal and glass. A clear rapprochement with rationalist criteria took place under the guise of a re-established tie with the ancient architectural tradition of the country. Among the first and more important works are the Reader's Digest complex, the Shinjō (temple), and the Nippon Gakki building, all three in Tokyo. A rationalist approach to structure was also tried in residential and domestic architecture.

On the whole, an architecture has emerged that is free of orthogonal rigidity and tends toward curvilinear or angular surfaces, divorced as much as possible from a concern for volume. The use of new materials has moreover permitted surfaces to be arranged in unforeseen perspectives, with combinations of discontinuous levels balanced on pillars. These new tendencies are also exemplified in the monumental complex of buildings at Hiroshima, the Ehime Convention Hall, and other structures designed by Kenzo Tange, one of the major exponents of modern Japanese architecture. But here we are dealing with an architecture of the summit, a display of showpieces that have little in common with the average building activity that determines the face of a city. It is a question of an avant-garde architecture, not only Japanese but worldwide, in search of aesthetic solutions (in recent years more plastic than linear, whence the substitution of glass-and-concrete for glass-and-metal). It is an architecture that, despite the growing resources of prefabrication, has few possibilities for application on a broad scale and tends to transform the architectural project into an industrial *design*.

The existing rupture between an elite architecture and the building trade is accentuated by the fact that Japan is surely one of the industrial countries that has invested least in public housing, which explains the lack of any true direction in the sphere of everyday architecture. This failure is also reflected in the area of city planning, where residential neighborhoods have ended by bearing no relation to the city as a whole. In addition, Japanese architects have been more concerned with areas of collective rather than individual life. They have turned their attention to stadiums and recreation centers, to university campuses, and above all have indulged in ideal city-planning projects in pursuit of a spectacular avant-garde vision that not infrequently confounds the future with utopia. This is true despite the fact that in recent decades a few organic approaches have been studied and in part carried out, especially for the unification of lesser urban centers, as in the case of

222. Totsuka, Golf Club, by Kenzo Tange.
223. Matsuyama, Ehime Convention Hall, by Kenzo Tange.

222. Totsuka, Golf Club, by Kenzo
Tange.
223. Matsuyama, Ehime Convention
Hall, by Kenzo Tange.

224. Tokyo, Catholic Center of St.
Mary's Cathedral, by Kenzo Tange.

Kita-Kyushu, formed by the merging of five cities, and the urban project to achieve a single great Osaka-Kobe metropolis. Tokyo itself is the prime example of such projects for the enlargement of the great metropolises: one of the plans presented foresees the city as constituting the geographic center of the plain of Kwanto in the near future, with the construction of a certain number of satellite cities in order to decentralize industry and other economic activities. A rapid transport system would link the satellite towns to each other and with Tokyo. The whole complex would constitute a Greater Tokyo, or the "metropolitan circle" of Japan. Another project, first offered in 1958 by Hisarō Kano, predicts a future development of the city as the capital of the nation and as an industrial, commercial, and maritime center for the whole Far East as well as for Japan. With this objective in mind, a radical exploitation of Tokyo Bay has been recommended, in order to reclaim an area of some 600 to 650 million square yards. Other plans have been developed to exploit Tokyo Bay, not through drainage and refill operations, but by constructing elevated or sea-level platforms supported on pillars or other structures set into the sea floor.

The plan offered by Kenzo Tange falls within the context of these studies. His overall scheme provides for a gradual reconstruction of the existing city and its progressive expansion into the bay area. The restructuring of the city would be carried out along an axis connected to various cyclical units constituting a complex of administrative centers. The civic axis would begin at the present metropolitan center and extend toward the bay. Constructions would be erected either on artificial platforms or on reclaimed land. The first, because of the greater guarantee of solidity and stability, would allow these areas to be developed vertically through multilevel structures; the second would call for a horizontal distribution of various building complexes. With the subway laid out along the civic axis, transportation could be easily dispatched from stations along a single line through a cyclical transport system on three levels, from the present center of the city to all points on the bay. The criterion substantially unfolded by the project is that of the necessity for the transition from a centripetal radial system to one of urban development in the linear sense. It promotes the combination in an organic unity of both the elements of urban planning and the architectural structures of the city, including the communications and transportation system. Finally, it aims at the realization of a new urban spatial order, one reflecting the organization and mobility of present society, of which present-day Tokyo is one of the most dramatic expressions, not only in Japan but in the entire world.

Adolfo Tamburello

225. Kamakura, Museum of Modern
Art, by Junzō Sakakura.

NOTES

Chapter Three

CHINA

[1] Laurence Sickman and Alexander Soper, *The Art and Architecture of China*, Baltimore 1956, p. 285.
[2] E. Biot, *Le Tcheou-li*, II, Paris 1851, pp. 555-56.
[3] Arthur Waley, *The Book of Songs*, London 1937, p. 33.
[4] Sickman and Soper, *op. cit.*, p. 207.
[5] *Ibid.*, p. 216.
[6] *Shih Chi*, VI, translated by E. Chavannes, "Les Mémoires historiques de Se-ma Ts'en," Paris 1895-1905.
[7] Imperial Ch'ing Encyclopedia: T'u Shu Chi Ch'eng, quoted in *Shui Ching Chu*.
[8] Sui Shu, Chap. LXVIII.
[9] San Tendai Godaisan Ki.
[10] A.C. Moule, *Quinsai, with Other Notes on Marco Polo*, Cambridge 1957.
[11] J. Fontein, "Cina storica," *Enciclopedia Universale dell'Arte*, VIII, Rome-Venice 1958, col. 638.
[12] Sickman and Soper, *op. cit.*, p. 283.
[13] "China's Architectural Heritage and Tasks of Today," in *People's China*, I, 21, November 1952.

SELECTED BIBLIOGRAPHY

HIMALAYAN REGION

General Works

Archaeological Survey of India, Report XXVI (Excavations in Kapilavastu), Part I, 1901.

BENOIT F., *L'Architecture: L'Orient médiéval et moderne,* Paris 1912.

BROWN F., *Indian Architecture,* Bombay 1965.

FERGUSSON J., *A History of Indian and Eastern Architecture,* London 1876.

ROWLAND B., *The Art and Architecture of India,* 3rd ed. Baltimore 1967.

VOLWAHSEN A., *Living Architecture: Indian,* New York 1969.

Kashmir

COWIE W.G., "Notes on Some of the Temples of Kashmir Especially Those Not Described by General Sunningham," *Journal of the Asiatic Society of Bengal,* XXXV, 1866.

GOETZ H., *Studies in the History and Art of Kashmir and the Indian Himalayas,* Wiesbaden 1969.

KAK R.C., *Ancient Monuments of Kashmir,* London 1933.

SAHNI D.R., "Excavations at Avantipur," *Archaeological Survey of India, Annual Report,* 1913-1914, p. 40.

SAHNI D.R., "Pre-Muhammadan Monuments of Kashmir," *Archaeological Survey of India, Annual Report,* 1915-1914, pp. 49-78.

Nepal

BROWN P., "The Art of Nepal," *Journal of the Bihar Research Society,* XXXI, 1945.

KARAN P. and JENKINS W.M., *The Himalayan Kingdoms: Bhutan, Sikkim and Nepal,* Princeton 1963.

LÜBKE H., *Kunst aus dem Königreich von Himalaya,* Villa Hügel-Hessen 1967.

SNELLGROVE D.L., "Nepal," *Splendors of the East,* New York 1965.

SNELLGROVE D.L., "Shrines and Temples of Nepal," *Arts Asiatiques,* 1961.

TUCCI G., "Note e appunti di un viaggio nel Nepal," *Bollettino della Società Geografica Italiana,* LXVIII, 1937.

WALDSCHMIDT E. and R.L., *Nepal (Art Treasures from the Himalayas),* London 1969.

Tibet

FRANCKE A.M., *Antiquities of Indian Tibet,* 2 vols., Calcutta 1914-1926.

GORDON A.K., *Tibetan Religious Arts,* New York 1952.

HUMMEL A., *Geschite der Tibetischen Kunst,* Leipzig 1953.

JISL L., *Tibetan Art,* London 1958.

RICHARDSON H.E., "Early Burial Grounds in Tibet and Tibetan Decorative Art of the VIII and IX Century," *Central Asiatic Journal,* VIII, 1963.

ROUSSEAU P., "L'Art du Tibet," *Revue des Arts Asiatiques,* IV, 1927.

TUCCI G., *A Lhasa e oltre. Diario della spedizione nel Tibet,* 2nd ed., Rome 1952.

TUCCI G., *Indo-tibetica,* 4 vols., Rome 1932-1941.

TUCCI G., "The Symbolism of the Temple of Bsam-yas," *East and West,* VI, 1955-1956.

TUCCI G., *Tibet: Paese delle nevi,* Novara 1968.

TUCCI G., *The Tombs of Tibetan Kings,* Rome 1950.

TUCCI G., *Tra giungle e pagode,* Rome 1953.

CENTRAL ASIA

AL'BAUM L.I., *Balalyk tepe,* Tashkent 1960.

BELENICKIJ A.M., *et al. Skultura i zivopis' drevnego Pjandzikenta,* Moscow 1959.

BUSSAGLI M., *Culture e civiltà dell'Asia Centrale,* Rome 1970.

BUSSAGLI M., "Culture protostoriche e arte delle steppe," *Civiltà dell'Oriente,* Rome 1961.

BUSSAGLI M., *Painting of Central Asia,* Geneva 1963.

ESIN E., *Antecedents and Development of Buddhist and Manichaean Turkish Art in Eastern Turkestan and Kansu,* Istanbul 1967.

FRUMKIN G., *Archaeology in Soviet Central Asia,* Leyden 1970.

GRÜNWDEL A., *Alt-Kutscha,* Berlin 1920.

HACKIN J., "Recherches archéologiques en Asie Centrale (1931)," *Revue des Arts Asiatiques,* IX, 1936.

HACKIN J. and CARL J., "Nouvelles Recherches archéologiques à Bamiyan," *Mémoires de la Délégation Archéologique Française en Afghanistan,* III, 1933.

HAMBIS L., "Asia Centrale," *E.U.A.,* II, Rome-Venice 1958, cols. 1-25.

JAKBUOVSKIJ A.J., *et al. Zipovis' drevnego Pjandzikenta,* Moscow 1954.

LAVROV V.A., *Gradostroitelnaja kul'tura Srednej Asii,* Moscow 1950.

LE COQ A. VON, *Bilderatlas zur Kunst und Kulturgeschichte Mittelasiens,* Berlin 1925.

LITVINSKY B.A. and ZEIMAL T.J., *Adzina tepa,* Moscow 1971.

MASSON V.M., *Srednjaja Azija i Drevjij Vostok,* Moscow-Leningrad 1964.

PUGACENKOVA G.A. and REMPEL L.I., *Istorija iskusstv Uzbekistan,* Moscow 1965.

SARIANIDI V.I., "Nekotorye voprosy drevnej architeltury eneoliticeskich poselenij geoksjurskogo oazisa," *Bulletin of Researches of the Institute of Material Culture,* 91, Moscow

1962.

SISKIN V.A., *Varachsa*, Moscow 1953.

STEIN A., *Ancient Khotan*, 2 vols., Oxford 1907.

STEIN A., *Ruins of Desert Cathay, a Personal Narrative of Exploration in Central Asia*, 2 vols., London 1912.

STEIN A., *Serindia*, 5 vols., Oxford 1921.

TALBOT RICE T., *Ancient Arts of Central Asia*, London 1965.

TOLSTOV S.P., *Drevnij Chorezm*, Moscow 1948.

TOLSTOV S.P.,*Po sledam drevnichorezmijskoj civilizacii*, Moscow-Leningrad 1948.

TOLSTOV S.P. and BAINBERG B.I., *Koj-krylgan-kala*, Moscow 1967.

CHINA

General Works

BOERSCHMANN E., *Baukunst und Landschaft in China*, Berlin 1923.

BOERSCHMANN E., *Die Baukunst und religiöse Kultur der Chinesen: Pagoden*, Berlin-Leipzig 1911-1931.

BOERSCHMANN E., *Chinesische Architektur*, Berlin 1925.

BOYD A., *Chinese Architecture and Town Planning, 1500 B.C.-A.D. 1911*, Chicago 1962.

CHANG KWANG-CHIH, *The Archaeology of Ancient China*, London-New Haven 1963.

CHAVANNES E., *Mission archéologique dans la Chine septentrionale*, 5 vols., Paris 1913-1915.

CHENG TE-K'UN, *Archaeology in China*, 4 vols., Cambridge, Eng. 1958-1966.

CREE H.G., *The Birth of China*, London 1936; new ed., New York 1954.

EBERHARD W., "Temple-Building Activities in Medieval and Modern China, An Experimental Study," *Monumenta Serica*, XXIII, 1964, pp. 264-318.

FUGL-MEYER H., *Chinese Bridges*, Shanghai 1937.

GIN-DIJH SU, *Chinese Architecture—Past and Contemporary*, Hong Kong 1964.

GLEN T.T., "Chinese Cities, Origins and Functions," *Annals of the Association of American Geographers*, XLII, 1952.

GROUSSET R., *La Chine et son art*, Paris 1951.

HALLADE M., *L'Asie du Sud-est*, Paris 1954.

HENTZE C., *Funde in Alt China*, Göttingen-Zurich, Berlin-Frankfurt 1967.

INN H and LU S., *Chinese Houses and Gardens*, Honolulu 1940.

JENYNS S. and ECKE G., *Chinese Domestic Furniture*, Peking 1944.

JIRO M., *Manshu no Shieki*, Tokyo 1944.

KELLING R., *Das Chinesische Wohnhaus*, Tokyo 1925.

LIU HSIAO-P'ING, *Chung-kuo Chienchu Lei-shing Chi Chieh-kon*, Peking 1957.

LIU TUN-CHEN, *Ching-kuo Chu-chai K'ai huo*, Peking 1957.

LIU TUN-CHEN, "Domestic Houses, Origins," *Chien-chi-hsueh pao*, No. 4, 1956.

MAKITA I., *Jukka koseki to Chibetto Bijutsu*, Tokyo 1943.

MIRAMS D.G., *A Brief History of Chinese Architecture*, Shanghai 1940.

MORTARI VERGARA CAFFARELLI, P., "Cina," *Dizionario di Architettura e urbanistica*, I, 1968, pp. 568-583.

MO TSUN-CH'ANG, "Architectural Decoration," *China Reconstructs*, IV, 9, 1955.

MÜNSTERBERG H., *L'Arte dell'Estremo Oriente*, Milan 1968.

PIROZZOLI M. and SERSTEVENS T., *Living Architecture: China*, New York 1971.

PRIP-MØLLER J., *Chinese Buddhist Monasteries*, Copenhagen-London 1937.

SICKMAN L. and SOPER A., *The Art and Architecture of China*, 2nd ed., Baltimore 1960.

SIRÉN O., "Les Capitales chinoises de l'ouest," *Japon et Extrême-Orient*, November-December 1924.

SIRÉN O., "Chinese Architecture," *Encyclopaedia Britannica*, 14th ed.

SIRÉN O., *Gardens in China*, New York 1949.

SIRÉN O., *Histoire des arts anciens de la Chine*, Vol. IV (*L'Architecture*), Paris-Brussels 1929-1930.

SPEISER W., GOEPPER R. and FRIBOURG J., *Arts de la Chine*, Vol. II, Freiburg 1963.

SWANN P.C., *L'Arte della Cina*, Florence 1966.

TOKIWA D., and SEKINO T., *Shina Bukkyō Shiseki*, 5 vols., Tokyo 1926-1938.

WALEY A., *The Temple*, London 1923.

WANG-PI-WEN, *Chung-kuo Chienchu*, Peking 1943.

WILLETTS W., *Chinese Art*, 2 vols., London 1958.

WU N., *Chinese and Indian Architecture*, New York 1963.

YAO CH'ENG-TSU, CHANG CHIH-KANG and LIU TUN-CHEN, *Ying-tsao Fa-yuan*, Peking 1959.

YETTS W.P., "Writings in Chinese Architecture," *Burlington Magazine*, March 1927.

Protohistory and the Shang Dynasty

CHENG TE-K'UN, "The Origin and Development of Shang Culture," *Asia Major*, VI, 1957, pp. 80-90.

EBERHARD W., "Bericht über die Ausgrabungen bei An-yang (Honan)," *Ostasiatische Zeitschrift*, New Series, VIII, 1-2, 1932.

HASKIN F.J., "Pan-p'o, a Chinese Neolithic Village," *Artibus Asiae*, XX, 1957, pp. 151-158.

LOEHR M., "The Stratigraphy of Hsiao-t'un (Anyang)," *Ars Orientalis*, II, 1957, pp. 439-457.

SHIH CHANG-Ju, "Hsiao-t'un, I: The Site; II: Architectural Remains," *Archaeologia Sinica*, 1959.

Chou Dynasty

Ch'ang-sha fa-chueh pao-kao, Peking 1957.

CHENG TE-K'UN, *Archaeological Studies in Szechwan*, Cambridge, Eng. 1957.

CHIANG YUEN-YI, *Ch'ang-sha, The Ch'u Tribe and Its Arts*, 2 vols., Shanghai 1949-1950.

HAN-TAN, "Excavations at the Ruins of the Capital of Chao in the Contending States Period," *Archaeologia Orientalis*, Series B, VII.

HASKIN F.J., "Recent Excavations in China," *Archives of the Chinese Art Society of America*, X, 1956.

KARLBECK O., "Notes on a Huihsien Tomb," *Röhsska Konstslöjdmuseet*, Arstryck 1952, pp. 40-47.

SEKINO T., "Investigations of Lintzu of Ch'i," *Kokogaku Zasshi*, XXXII, 1942.

SOOTHIL W.E., *The Hall of Light*, London 1951.

WANG KUO-WEI, "Ming-t'ang miao ch'in t'ung k'ao" (German translation by J. Hefter), *Ostasiatische Zeitschrift*, New Series, VII, 1-2, 1931.

Ch'in and Han Dynasties

CHENG TE-K'UN, *Archaeological Studies in Szechwan*, Cambridge, Eng. 1957.

FAIRBANCS W., "The Offering Shrines of Wu Liang Tz'u," *Harvard Journal of Asiatic Studies*, 6, 1941, pp. 1-36.

FRANKE W., "Die Han-zeitlichen Felsengräber bei Chia-ting, West Szechuan," *Studia Serica*, VII, 1951.

GEIL W.E., *The Great Wall of China*, London 1909.

LARTIGUE J., "Au Tombeau de Houo K'iu-Ping," *Artibus Asiae*, II, 1927, pp. 85-94.

LARTIGUE J., "Résultats archéologiques," *Journal Asiatique*, May-June 1961, p. 407.

LIU TUNG-TSENG, "Ta-chuang Shih Notes," *Chung'kuo Ying tsao Hsueh She Hui-k'an*, 1932, pp. 130-133.

MIYAZAKI I., "Les Villes en Chine à l'époque des Han," *T'oung Pao*, XLVIII, 1960, 4-5, pp. 1-18.

MORI O., and NAITO H., "Ying-ch'eng-tzu," *Archaeologia Orientalis*, IV, 1934.

NEWTON HAYES J., *The Great Wall of China*, Shanghai 1929.

RUDOLPH R.C. and WEN YU, *Han Tomb Art of West China*, Los Angeles-Berkeley 1951.

SEGALEN V., DE VOISINS G. and LARTIGUE J., *L'art funéraire à l'époque des Han*, Paris 1936.

SEKINO T., "Ancient Chinese Stone Shrines," *Kokka*, 225, February 1909.

SEKINO T., "The Site of the Ling-Kuang Hall of Lum in the Former Han," *Kokogaku Zasshi*, XXXI, 1940.

SEKINO T., "Stone Mortuary Shrines with Engraved Tablets of the Later Han Dynasty," *Kokka*, 225, February 1909.

WHITE W.C., *The Tombs of Old Lo-yang*, Shanghai 1934.

Six Dynasties

BUHOT J., "Notes d'architecture bouddhique, I: Stupa et pagode, une hypothèse," *Revue des Arts Asiatiques*, XI, 4, 1937.

CHANG SHU-HUNG, "Tun-huang Memoirs," *China Reconstructs*, IX, 2, 1960.

CHU HSI-TSU, *et al.*, "The Tombs of the Six Dynasties," *Monumenta Sinica*, I, Nanking 1935.

GRAY B. and VINCENT J.B., *Buddhist Cave Paintings at Tun-huang*, London 1959.

LO SHU-TZU, *Pei Ch'ao shih-k'u i-shu*, Shanghai 1955.

MIZUNO S. and NAGAHIRO T., *A study of the Buddhist Cave Temples at Lungmen, Honan*, Tokyo 1941.

MIZUNO S. and NAGAHIRO T., *Yung-kang, the Buddhist Cave Temples of the Fifth Century A.D. in North China*, Kyoto 1952 ff.

PELLIOT P., *Les Grottes de Touen-Houang*, Paris 1920-1924.

SUI KAO-JOUAN, "Tch'ong-k'an Lo-yang K'u lan ki, T'ai pei," *Academia Sinica*, 1960.

SULLIVAN M., *The Cave Temples of Maichishan*, London 1969.

WARE J., "Wei shou on Buddhism," *T'oung Pao*, XXX, 1933.

Wen-wu ts'an-k'ao tz'u-hao, 3, 1956, pp. 62-64.

Sui and T'ang Dynasties

ADACHI K., *Chao-an shiseki mo kenkyū*, Tokyo 1933.

BULLING A., "Buddhist Temples in the T'ang Period," *Oriental Art*, I, 2, 1955, pp. 79-86; 3, pp. 115-122.

CHENG TE-K'UN, "The Royal Tomb of Wang Chien," *Harvard Journal of Asiatic Studies*, 8, 1944-1945, pp. 235-240.

CHOBU HIBINO, *Godaisan (Wu-t'ai-shan)*, Tokyo 1942.

Chung-kuo chien-chu, Peking 1957.

FEN HAN-YI, "Discovery and Excavation of the Yung Ling," *Archives of the Chinese Art Society of America*, 2, 1947, pp. 11-20.

FISCHER W., *The Sacred Wu-t'ai-shan*, London 1925.

LIANG S.C., "The Great Stone Bridge of Chao Hsien (Hopeh)," *Chung-kuo Ting-tsao Hsueh She Hui-k'an*, 1, 1934, pp. 1-31.

SIRÉN O., "Tch'ang-ngan au temps des Souei et des T'ang," *Revue des Arts Asiatiques*, 1-2, March 1927, pp. 40-46, 98-104.

SOPER A.C., "A Vacation Glimpse of the T'ang Temples of Ch'ang-an, the Ssu-t'a chi by Tuan Ch'eng shih," *Artibus Asiae*, XXIII, 1960, pp. 15-40.

SULLIVAN M.D., "The Excavations of a T'ang Imperial Tomb," *Illustrated London News*, April 20, 1946.

T'ang Ch'ang-an Ta-ming kung, Peking 1959.

TWITCHETT D., "Some Remarks on Irrigation Under the T'ang," *T'oung Pao*, XLVIII, 1-3, 1960, pp. 175-194.

WRIGHT A.F., "Symbolism and Function: Reflections on Changan and Other Great Cities," *Journal of Asiatic Study*, XXIV, 4, 1965.

Liao Dynasty

LIANG S.C., "Two Liao Structures of Tu-lo Ssu, Chi Hsien, Hopei," *Bulletin of the Society for Research in Chinese Architecture*, III, 2, 1932, pp. 48-88.

NAKAMURA R., *Manshu no Bijutsu*, Tokyo 1941.

SEKINO T. and TAKEJIMA T., *Ryōkin Jidau no Kenckiku to sono Butsuzō*, 2 vols., Tokyo 1925-1944.

TAMURA J. and KOBAYSHI Y., *Tombs and Mural Paintings of Ch'ing-ling, Liao Imperial Mausoleums of the Eleventh Century A.D. in Eastern Mongolia*, Kyoto 1953.

Sung Dynasty

DEMIÉVILLE, P. "Review of 1920 Edition of the Ying Tsao Fa Shih," *B.E.F.E.O.*, XXV, 1925.

ECKE G. and DEMIÉVILLE P., *The Twin Pagodas of Zayton*, Cambridge, Mass. 1935.

MOULE A.C., *Quinsai, with Other Notes of Marco Polo*, Cambridge 1957.

Ta-tsu shih-k'o, Peking 1957.

YETTS W., "Review of 1925 Edition of the Ying Tsao Fa Shih," *Bulletin of the School of Oriental and African Studies*, IV, 1926-1928.

Yüan, Ming, and Ch'ing Dynasties

ARLINGTON L.C. and LEWISON W., *In Search of Old Peking*, Peking 1935.

CANG CHUNG-I, TS'AO CHIEN-PIN and CH'UAN KAO-CHIEH, *Hui-chon Ming-fai Chu-chai*, Peking 1957.

HOU JEN-CHIH, "Peking: Historical Sketch," *People's China*, October 1956.

JIRO M., *Manshū no Shiseki*, Tokio 1944.

KOKU YAO LUN, *The Essential Criteria of Antiquities for Chinese Connoisseurship*, London 1971.

LANCASTER C., "The European-Style Palaces of the Yüan Ming Yüan," *Gazette des Beaux-Arts*, October 1948.

LING SSU-CH'ENG, *Ching Shih Ying-tsao Tse-li*, Peking 1934.

MAKITA I., *Jukka koseki to Chibetto Bijutsu*, Tokyo 1943.

MALONE C.B., *History of the Peking Summer Palaces Under the Ch'ing Dynasty*, New York 1966.

NAI HSIA, "Opening an Imperial Tomb," *China Reconstructs*, VII, 3, 1959, pp. 16-21

SIRÉN O., *The Imperial Palaces of Peking*, 3 vols., Paris-Brussels 1926.

SIRÉN O., *The Walls and Gates of Peking*, London 1924.

SKINNER R.T.F., "Peking, 1953," *The Architectural Review*, October 1953.

YOSHIKI O., "Architecture of the Central Edifice in the Imperial Palace in Ancient China," *Paleologia*, XI, 1, 1962.

Modern Period

CHEN C., "Modern Chinese Architecture," *The Architectural Review*, July 1947.

COLLOTTI PISCHEL E., "Città e campagna nella Cina contemporanea," *Controspazio*, 1, January-February 1971.

GAVINELLI C. and VERCELLONI V., eds. "Cina: Architettura e urbanistica," *Controspazio*, 12, December 1971.

LIANG SSU-CH'ENG, "China's Architectural Heritage and the Tasks of Today," *People's China*, I, 21, November 1952.

PEN C., "Chinese Vernacular Architecture," *The Journal of the Royal Institute of British Architects*, LXXII (1965), 10, pp. 502-507.

KOREA

General Works

Chōsen Kōseki Zufu (Korean Antiquities Illustrated), 15 vols., Seoul 1915-1935.

CLARK C.A., *Religion of Old Korea*, New York 1932.

DALLET C., *Histoire de l'église de la Corée*, 2 vols., Paris 1874.

DUPONT M., *Décoration coréenne*, Paris 1927.

ECKHARDT A., *A History of Korean Art*, London 1929.

FERNALD H.E., "Rediscovered Glories of Korean Art," *Asia*, December 1931, pp. 788-795, 799-802.

FUJISHIMA G., *Chōsen Kenchiku Shiron* (History of Korean Architecture), Tokyo 1930.

GALE J.A., *History of the Korean People*, Seoul 1927.

GOMPERTZ G. ST. G.M., "Arte della Corea," *Civiltà dell'Oriente*, IV, Rome 1962, pp. 1243-1267.

GOMPERTZ G. ST. G.M., "Corea, Coreani centri e tradizioni," *E.U.A.*,

III, Rome-Venice 1958, cols. 800-801.

GRIFFIS W.E., *Corea, the Hermit Kingdon*, New York 1911.

GRISWOLD A.B., KIM C. and POTT P.H., *Birmania, Korea, Tibet*, Milan 1963.

HAYASHI T., *Chōsen tsū-shi* (History of Korea), Tokyo 1944.

HULBERT H.R., *The History of Korea*, 2 vols., Seoul 1905.

HULBERT H.R., *The Passing of Korea*, New York 1906.

KEITH E. and ROBERTSON SCOTT E.K., *Old Korea*, London 1946.

KIM C., ed. *The Culture of Korea*, Los Angeles 1946.

"The Korean National Commission for UNESCO," *UNESCO Korean Survey*, Seoul 1960.

Kōseki Chōsa Hōkoku (Annual Reports of the Exploration of Ancient Ruins), 20 vols., Seoul 1917-1940.

Kōseki Chōsa Tokubetsu Hokoku (Special Reports on the Exploration of Ancient Ruins), 6 vols., Seoul 1919-1930.

LAUTENSACH H., *Korea: Land, Volk, Schicksal*, Stuttgart 1950.

LAUTENSACH H., *Korea, eine Landeskunde auf Grund einige Reisen und der Literatur*, Leipzig 1945.

LONGFORD J.H., *The Story of Korea*, London 1911.

McCUNE E., *The Arts of Korea: An Illustrated History*, Rutland-Tokyo 1962.

McKENZIE F.A., *The Tragedy of Korea*, London 1908.

MÜNSTERBERG H., *L'Arte dell'estremo Oriente*, Milan 1968.

OSGOOD C., *The Koreans and Their Culture*, New York 1951.

ROSS J., *Korea: Its History, Manners and Customs*, Paisley 1880.

ROSSETTI C., *Corea e Coreani*, Milan 1906.

SEKINO T., *Chōsen Bijutsu-shi* (His-

tory of Korean Art), Kyoto 1932.

SEKINO T., *Chōsen no Kenchiku to Geijutsu* (Art and Architecture in Korea: Collection of Essays), Tokyo 1942.

SEKINO T., *Kenkoku kenchiku chōsa Hōkoku* (Report of Research on Korean Architecture), Tokyo 1904.

STARR F., *Korean Buddhism: History, Condition, Art*, Boston 1918.

UMEHARA S., *Chōsen Kodai no Bosei* (Funeral Customs of Ancient Korea), Tokyo 1947.

WON-YONG KIM, *et al.*, *Korean Arts, III: Architecture*, Ministry of Public Information, Republic of Korea 1963.

YANAGI S., *Chōsen to Sono Geijutsu* (Korea and Its Art Treasures), Tokyo 1922; reprinted 1954.

Prehistory

TORII R., "Les Dolmens de la Corée," *Memoirs of the Research Department*, Tokyo Bunko, I, 1926, pp. 93-100.

UMEHARA S., *Chōsen Kodai no Bunko* (The Ancient Culture of Korea), Kyoto 1946.

Lo-Lang Colony

HARASA Y. and TAZAWA K., *Lo-lang*, Tokyo 1930.

IKEUCHI H., "A Study on Lo-lang and Taifang, Ancient Chinese Prefectures in the Korean Peninsula," *Memoirs of the Research Department*, Tokyo Bunko, Series B, 5, 1930, pp. 79-96.

KOIZUM A., *The Tomb of Painted Baskets of Lo-lang*, Seoul 1934.

OBA T. and KAYAMOTO K., *The Tomb of Wang Kuang of Lo-lang*, Seoul 1935.

SEKINO T., *et al.*, "Rakuro-gun Jidai no Iseki" (Research on the Lo-lang District), *Koseki Chosa Tokubetsu Hokoku*, 1-3, 1925-1927.

UMEHARA S., "Two Remarkable

Lo-lang Tombs of Wooden Construction Excavated in Pyongyang, Korea," *Archives of the Chinese Art Society of America*, VIII, 1954, pp. 10-21.

Three Kingdoms Period

CHAPIN H.B., and YO PU, "One of Korea's Ancient Capitals," *Transactions of the Korea Branch of the Royal Asiatic Society*, XXXII, 1951, pp. 51-61.

CHAVANNES E., "Rapport sur les monuments de l'ancien royaume coréen de Kao-keou-li, *Comptes rendus des séances de l'Académie des Inscriptions et Belles-lettres*, 1906, p. 549.

Chōsen Kofun Hekiga-shu (Wall Paintings in Ancient Koguryo Tombs), Seoul 1917.

COURANT M., "Stèle chinoise du royaume de Ko Kou Rya," *Journal Asiatique*, IX, 1899, pp. 210-239.

IKEUCHI H. and UMEHARA S., *T'ung-kou*, 2 vols., Tokyo, 1938-1940.

KIM C., "Two Old Silla Tombs," *Artibus Asiae*, X, 1947.

KIM C., *Two Old Silla Tombs*, Seoul 1948.

SEKINO T., *et al.*, "Kōkuri Jidai no Iseki" (Research on Koguryo), *Kōseki Chōsa Tokubetsu Hōkoku* (Special Reports of Research on Antiquity), 1-2, Tokyo 1938-1940.

UMEHARA S., "The Newly Discovered Tombs with Wall Paintings of the Kao-kou-li Dynasty," *Archives of the Chinese Art Society of America*, VI, 1952, pp. 5-17.

Great Silla Kingdom

CHAPIN H.B., "A Hitherto Unpublished Great Silla Pagoda," *Artibus Asiae*, XII, 1-2, 1949, pp. 84-138.

CHAPIN H.B., "Kyongju, Ancient Capital of Silla," *Asian Horizon*, I, 4, 1948, pp. 36-45.

Chōsen Hobotsu Koseki Zuroku (Illustrated Catalogue of Korean Treasures and Remains), Vol. I, Seoul 1938-1940.

COURANT M., "Korea up to the Ninth Century," *T'oung P'ao*, Series I, IX, Paris 1899.

HAMADA K. and UMEHARA S., "Keishu Kinkantsuka to Sono Iho" (The Golden Crown Tomb at Kyongju and Its Treasures), *Koseki Chōsa Tokubetsu Hokoku*, 1-3, 1924-1927.

KIM C., and KIM W. and P., *Excavations of Three Silla Tombs*, Seoul 1955.

OGAWA K., and BABA K., "Ryosan Fufu Tsuka to Sono Ibutsu" (The Tomb of the Couple at Yangsan and Its Remains), *Koseki Chōsa Tokubetsu Hōkoku*, 1-2, 1927.

YUSOP KO, *Chōsen T'ap-p'a ni Yongu* (History of Korean Pagodas), Seoul 1948.

Koryo Kingdom

FUJISHIMA G., *Chōsen no Kenchiku to Geijutsu* (Art and Architecture of Korea), Tokyo 1942.

VIESSMAN W., "Ondol Radiant Heat in Korea," *Transactions of the Korea Branch of the Royal Asiatic Society*, XXXI, 1948-1949.

Li Dynasty

CHAPIN H.B., "Palaces in Seoul," *Transactions of the Korea Branch of the Royal Asiatic Society*, XXXII, 1951, pp. 3-46.

GRAJDANZEV A.J., *Modern Korea*, New York 1933.

KUNO Y.S., *Japanese Expansion on the Asiatic Continent*, Berkeley 1937-1940.

McCUNE E., *Korea's Heritage: A Regional and Social Geography*, Tokyo 1956.

McCUNE E. and GREY A.L., *Korea Today*, Cambridge, Mass. 1950.

PARK L.G., *The History of Protestant Missions in Korea, 1910-1932*, Pyongyang 1929.

JAPAN

General Works

ALEX W., *Japanese Architecture*, New York 1963.

AMANUMA A., *Nihon Kenchiku Saibu Hensen Shozuroku* (Structural Transformations in Japanese Architecture), Tokyo 1944.

AMANUMA A., *Nihon Kenchiku Zuroku* (Illustrated Treatise on Japanese Architecture), 6 vols., Tokyo 1933-1939.

BALTZEN F., *Die Architektur der Kultbauten Japans*, Berlin 1904-1905.

DREXLER A., *The Architecture of Japan*, New York 1955.

GROPIUS W., *Architettura in Giappone*, Milan 1965.

ISHIWARA K., *Nihon Nomin Kenchiku* (Japanese Rural Architecture), 12 vols., Tokyo 1934-1939.

ITO C., INUI K., and OKUMA Y., *Meiji-zen Nihon Kenchiku Gijutsu-shi* (History of Japanese Architecture Before the Meiji Era), Tokyo 1961.

ŌTA H., *Japanese Architecture and Gardens*, Tokyo 1966.

PAINE R.T. and SOPER A.C., *The Art and Architecture of Japan*, 2nd ed. Baltimore 1960.

SADLER A.L., *A Short History of Japanese Architecture*, Sydney-London 1941.

SEKINO T., *Nihon no Kenchiku to Geijutsu* (Japanese Arts and Architecture), Tokyo 1940.

TAMBURELLO A., *I grandi monumenti del Giappone*, Milan 1971.

TAUT B., *Houses and Peoples of Japan*, Tokyo 1937.

YOSHIDA T., *Japanische Architektur*, Tübingen 1952.

Prehistory and Protohistory

KIDDER J.E., *Japan Before Buddhism*, London 1959.

TANGE K., KAWAZOE N., and WATANABE Y., *Ise-Nihon Kenchiku no Genkei* (The Origins of Japanese Architecture), Tokyo 1962.

Shinto and Buddhist Architecture

AKIYAMA A., *Shinto and Its Architecture*, Tokyo 1955.

BLASER W., *Japanese Temples and Tea-Houses*, New York 1957.

PONSONBY-FANE R.A.B., *Studies in Shinto and Shrines*, Kyoto 1942.

SOPER A.C., *The Evolution of Buddhist Architecture in Japan*, Princeton 1942.

Nara and Heian Periods

ASANO K., *Horyuji Kenchiku Sokan* (Architectural Splendors of the Horyuji), Kyoto 1953.

FUJIOKA, *Kyoto gosho* (The Imperial Palace of Kyoto), Kyoto 1955.

SANSOM G., "The Heian Capital and Its Palaces," *A History of Japan to 1334*, Stanford 1958.

Kamakura and Muromachi Periods

KITAO M., *Shoin Shosai Zufu* (Structural Elements of the Shoin-zukuri), Tokyo 1955.

ŌTA H., *Chusei no Kenchiku* (Medieval Architecture), Tokyo 1957.

TOYAMA E., *Muromachi-jidai Teienshi* (History of the Garden in the Muromachi Period), Tokyo 1934.

Momoyama and Yedo (Tokugawa) Periods

GROPIUS A. and TANGE K., *Katsura—Tradition and Creation in Japanese Architecture*, New Haven 1960.

HALL J.W., "The Castle Town and Japan's Modern Urbanization," *Far Eastern Quarterly*, XV, 1, 1955, pp. 37-56.

HORIGUCHI S., *Katsura Rikyu* (The Katsura Detached Palace), Tokyo 1952.

HORIGUCHI S., *Rikyu no Chashitsu* (The Teahouse of Rikyu), Tokyo 1952.

KITAO M., *Sukiya Shosai Zufu* (Structural Elements of the Sukiya Style), Tokyo 1955.

MORI O., *Katsura Rikyu* (The Katsura Detached Palace), Tokyo 1955.

Gardens

NAOYA S. and MOTOI H., *A Pictorial Record of the Famous Palaces, Gardens and Tea Gardens*, Tokyo 1935.

NEWSOM S., *A. Thousand Years of Japanese Gardens* Tokyo 1957.

TAMURA T., *Art of the Landscape Garden in Japan*, Tokyo 1935.

YOSHINAGA Y., *Nihon no Teien* (The Japanese Garden), Tokyo 1958.

YOSHINAGA Y., *Nihon Teien no Kosei to Hyogen* (Character and Expression of the Japanese Garden), Tokyo 1962.

Modern Period

ABE K., "Meiji Architecture," *Japanese Arts and Crafts in the Meiji Era*, Tokyo 1958.

BOYD R., *Orientamenti nuovi nell'architettura giapponese*, Milan 1969.

HORIKOSHI S., *Meiji shoki no Yofu Kenchiku* (Western-Style Architecture in the First Period of the Meiji Era), Tokyo 1929.

KOIKE S., *Nihon no Gendai Kenchiku* (Modern Japanese Architecture), Tokyo 1954.

TEMPEL E., *Nuova Architettura giapponese*, Milan 1969.

LIST OF PHOTOGRAPHIC CREDITS
The numbers refer to the plates

Arai Masao, Shinkenchiku-Sha, Tokyo: 201, 202, 203, 207, 212, 223

Archaeological Survey of India, Government of India: 27, 28, 29, 30, 31

Borromeo, Federico, Milano: I, II, III, IV, V, VI, VII, VIII, IX, X, XI, XII, XIII, XIV, XV, XVI, XVII, XVIII, XIX, XX, XXI, XXII, XXIII, XXIV

British Museum, London: 56, 90

Futagawa Yukio, Tokyo: 205, 208, 209, 210, 215, 216, 217, 218, 219

Kawasumi Akyo, Tokyo: 220, 221, 222

Lauros-Giraudon, Paris: 11, 12, 13, 19, 22, 23, 24, 25

Len Sirman Press, Geneva: 14, 15, 16, 17, 18, 20, 21, 50, 53, 54, 55, 67, 68, 70, 88, 90, 111, 113, 114, 118, 119, 122, 123, 124, 125, 129, 130, 131, 133, 134, 155, 156, 159, 160, 161, 163

Mele Pietro Francesco, Rome: 32, 34, 35, 36, 37, 38

Missi-Photo, Paris: 128, 146, 147, 153, 154

Musée Guimet, Paris: 71, 78, 107, 108, 109, 115, 116, 140, 145, 146, 147, 157

Museum of Fine Arts, Boston: 98

National Museum, Tokyo: 196, 197, 198

Nelson Gallery of Art, Kansas City: 59

Ogawa Taisuke, Shinkenchiku-Sha, Tokyo: 211, 224, 225

Photographic Service. The Metropolitan Museum, New York: 60

Royal Ontario Museum, Toronto: 58

Siren Archives, Östasiatiska Museet, Stockholm: 50, 61, 63, 64, 65, 66, 69, 79, 80, 81, 82, 83, 84, 85, 86, 87, 89, 92, 93, 95, 96, 97, 99, 100, 106, 112, 117, 120, 121, 126, 127, 132, 135, 136, 141, 142, 143, 144, 145, 148, 149, 150, 151, 152, 158, 160